self-help

ARE YOU **EMPOWERED**???
—the BASICS

by
Cynthia Lynn

GET THE

ACTION PLAN for FINANCIAL WELLNESS and A BETTER LIFE

READ ON...

Daccord Press

Albany New York

All rights reserved. No part of this publication may be reproduced or transmitted in any form or by any means, electronic or mechanical, including photocopy, recording, or any information storage and retrieval system, without permission in writing from the publisher.

For information about permission to reproduce selections from this book e-mail daccordpress@yahoo.com

Copyright © 2014 Cynthia Lynn

LCCN: 2014918072
ISBN-13: 978-0-989053648
ISBN-10: 0989053644

INTRODUCTION

Most consumers worldwide now believe that big business is in charge.

Cynthia Lynn wants all consumers to be confident that they can take **"action"** to initiate laws to be enacted by the legislative authorities of their country. And Americans must ask the United States Congress to offer more to consumers + add to the many government resources currently established to advise consumers in almost every situation of disagreement with a business that has infringed on a consumer's right to receive a product or service promised.

To this aim, **Cynthia Lynn** gives her non-USA readers examples of USA Federal/State websites and non-state others. Consumers worldwide must be proactive and ask their government to establish **"consumer help lines."** Consumers in foreign countries must also **encourage the Internet search engines available in their country** to make available sources for free information and expert researched advice about consumer related issues listing websites both "public access" as well as "ad sponsored."

Most importantly, this is a book that can benefit everyone no matter what country they live in.

Read on...

more about the author

CYNTHIA LYNN's writing experience includes specializing in travel writing. Her travel updates have been distributed to NPR stations, as well, she's been contributor to a number of travel related books and publications. Her print travel guides are in Libraries worldwide (WorldCat.Org). The first book *No More Hotels In Paris* was followed by *No More Hotels In*

Rome. The Paris book is still available in used copies sold on Amazon and the many excellent critic reviews included *Library Journal* and *The Philadelphia Inquirer*. Visit her website **www.cynthialynn.org** for more information about her books. See "screen clipping" below:

As well the Publisher of **Cynthia Lynn's** books Daccord Press has a website **www.daccordpress.com** where a description of her new E-book hub travel series can be found. See screen clipping below:

Cynthia Lynn's website is on the Authors Guild roster of published authors, she is a member of Authors Guild who maintains her website listed in Google and Yahoo, as well as other search engine sites.

MORE ABOUT ME AND HOW I BECAME EMPOWERED

I was a stringer for travel publications while I was employed as a marketing supervisor for an airline, and then I was recommended as a stringer to the managing Editor of a state wide weekly newspaper. I took the offer since I traveled state wide in the course of my work for the airline. Soon I was offered assignments by Editors of various state wide newspaper weeklies. I was able to do the research in public libraries. The topics were interesting and after a few years I learned how to sleuth out facts from public records in government agencies.

Of course, this was before the electronic age when writers like me developed persistence and honed our skill of researching for facts. After a while I could ferret out information about all kinds of business activities. Whatever I needed to discover was often in the public records. My research skill stood me in good stead whenever a predator business tried to cheat me out of what I paid for. I used my skills to find government agencies that could advise me about my rights as a consumer. And every time I succeeded in getting a refund or credit for the product or service I had paid for and didn't get, I was all the more EMPOWERED to keep track of how I spent my money. It wasn't long before I realized I had the power to make lifestyle changes and spend my money to enjoy my life.

Now I am passing on to my readers what I've learned about the way money controls our life style and how managing money can add to the measure of happiness.

Contents

	PAGE
Preface	11-2
SECTION ONE	13
The BASICS	14-5
What Does Empower Mean?	16
How To Take CONTROL OF YOUR LIFE	17-8
ACTION PLAN	19
You And Your Network	20-2
Federal Programs	23-5
YOUR Government Agencies	26-7
The Process of CHANGE	28-31
SECTION TWO	32
Pointers plus HOW-TO	33-4
INTERNET TIPS	35-7
"Consumer Advocates"	38-9
Consumer Friendly FED	40-1
Another Suggestion	42
The Sum Up	43
TEST Your Knowledge— QUESTIONS and ANSWERS	44-5
TOPIC 1. food Questions+ANSWERS A-B	46-9
TOPIC 2. mortgage (or rent) Questions+ANSWERS A-E	50-62
TOPIC 3. heating/cooling Questions+ANSWERS A-D	63-9
TOPIC 4. car Expenses Questions+ANSWERS A-E	70-78
TOPIC 5. health Insurance/other Questions+ANSWERS A-G	79-88
TOPIC 6. banking/credit-debit cards Questions+ANSWERS A-D	89-95

Contents-continued

PAGE

TOPIC 7. cell phone and/or landline
    Questions+ANSWERS A-D......96-100
TOPIC 8. TV/cable or satellite
    Questions+ANSWERS A-D.....101-105
TOPIC 9. Internet
    Questions+ANSWERS A-D.....106-109
TOPIC 10. clothes/other purchases
    Questions+ANSWERS A-D.....110-115
TOPIC 11. charity donations
    Questions+ANSWERS A-C......116-118
TOPIC 12. religious tithe
    Questions+ANSWERS A-C......119-122

SECTION THREE...............................123
How Did You Become
    Empowered........................124-5
INSPIRED to ACTION.......................126-7
Topics that NEED Consumer Action..128-9
selected "thinkingoutloudan"
    Blogs.....................130-155
the challenge to keep
    empowered...................156-7
INDEX..158-163
YOUR NOTES....................................164-5

ARE YOU EMPOWERED???   Cynthia Lynn

Preface

If you undertake this simple self-help step by step "how-to" take the path of "action" toward a better life, you are "climbing" toward the kind of self-knowledge leading to the "power" to take "action," and then you can become EMPOWERED to make many other life changes that once seemed impossible.

SECTION ONE starts this written step by step manual to explain the "WHY" of this book: a way to effect CHANGE with an "action plan."

SECTION TWO is for the benefit of all consumers in this global commerce 21st century who face the big business corporate powers free to sell inferior products and services in the marketplace. In this section are the TEST YOUR KNOWLEDGE series of QUESTIONS and ANSWERS providing examples of what all consumers in democratic countries need for resolution of a consumer issue based problem. The aim of this Section is to encourage all consumers everywhere to take "action" to ensure that there are government resources like those established in the USA for consumer protection in almost every situation of disagreement with a business that has infringed on a consumer's right to receive a product or service promised.

In this section I give my readers THE TOOLS to search for what they need to locate examples of what should be available in all democratic countries with free access availability "search engines" that provide unfettered access to official government website sources that have "consumer help lines" + "public access" and "AD sponsored" website sources for useful researched information by experts with solutions to specific consumer problems.

ARE YOU EMPOWERED??? Cynthia Lynn

SECTION THREE is entitled **Empowered,** and sums up Empowerment + the how to be inspired to more **ACTION**. Selected selections from my blog **www.thinkingoutloudan.blogspot.com** are also included in this section. See screen clipping below:

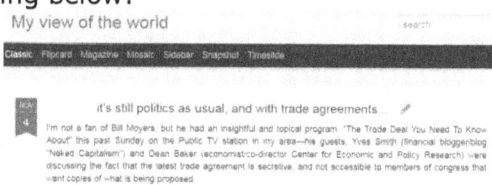

This is a consumer action blog aimed at encouraging "action contact" with your elected Federal/State/local Government representatives to offer your views about consumer issues that need legislation. I have other blogs too, for instance, I blog about words and meanings that have certain other definitions in this 21st century "politically correct" world we live in: **www.wordsplusmeanings.blogspot.com**
See "screen clipping" below:

Wordsandmeanings

SUNDAY, JULY 6, 2014

a word emotional and significant + more

The word bench has more than one significance, it also has an emotional connotation, as well a bench seats a certain kind of humanity who are often engaged, though they can be unengaged in what some do but there is a purpose for the bench in a certain kind of place.

I'm frequently involved in many book projects, also I have no specific blogging schedule, but I'll answer any comments or queries—do it at the above blogspot web addresses.

Read on...

SECTION ONE

The BASICS

HOW TO take CONTROL OF YOUR LIFE
and
ACTION PLAN

ARE YOU EMPOWERED??? Cynthia Lynn

The Basics

In countries around the world governments are intent on serving powerful interests, and it doesn't matter if your income is high or low, what you do to earn a living, or if you are retired, the 21st century global world is deliberately too complex with the intention of complex financial manipulations that make it difficult to analyze legitimate worth. The informational website examples given in this book are available in the USA, but such sites should be available in all Western democracies to citizens who are **Empowered** to demand it. Elsewhere it's necessary to employ an expert who ferrets out rules and regulations that may apply to a particular situation and then provides the client with a solution to the problem, because these citizens must cope with a civil service "rule driven" bureaucracy. It entails "move up the chain of command" to find someone who will offer a version of the correct interpretation of the "rule" that will get the best problem resolution.

All of the above effects 21st century global citizens and it's an effective damper as regards a better quality of life—the **EMPOWERED** can effect the necessary changes to make what once seemed impossible possible.

In the United States

Predatory big business and services providers are paying lobby groups to keep lawmakers from enacting any more consumer protections + using legal means to legislate away what little consumers can do about manufacturers that sell defective products. The impediments to effect a solution include contacting understaffed customer services stuck in the "leave a message" driven robotics. They are not deterred by Congress or anti-trust

ARE YOU EMPOWERED???   Cynthia Lynn

laws. Our Congressional legislators satisfy service provider lobby groups when they initiate laws with lobby group benefits interspersed with essential legislation overburdened with numerous extra clauses designed to please the lobby groups + their lawyers are employed to produce "too complex to read laws" passed by both houses of Congress without scrutiny, and ultimately signed by the President who is aware that the "K Street" lobby groups harness party politics with an endless supply of campaign donations and congressional perks.

Here's what US service providers have on their wish list: electric companies want to add to bonanza profits predicated by allowing them to charge for expenses related to maintenance of existing equipment; gas providers seek to limit or eliminate the regulatory need to apply for higher rates during unusual seasonal weather changes; global entity telephone providers of landlines in the USA are intent to pull the land wire to their existing customers with the end result of creating more customers for unregulated cell phone and cable phone telecommunications; internet providers are planning the opening of special Internet lanes for businesses that will pay more for faster service and keep the consumer from experiencing a truly unfettered web.

The end result of all of the above means USA consumers will have to suffer even more outrageous hikes of rates for service.

ARE YOU EMPOWERED???   Cynthia Lynn

what does EMPOWER mean?

THE "dictionary definition" of the word **EMPOWER** is "first and foremost: **to give power.** Another meaning for this word refers to **a lawyer or some legal authority YOU personally** give the **power** to **represent YOU**.

It doesn't matter if **YOU** have plenty of disposable income, or whether **YOU** pinch pennies to set your budget for the month, if **YOU** feel cheated because you didn't get what you paid for **YOU** need to **give power to YOURSELF to be EMPOWERED to take control of YOUR life.**

With this **STEP BY STEP** be **EMPOWERED** get **results** it's easy to learn **how to** harness and saddle up **YOUR Federal, State, Local government and/or "Government" civil service bureaucracy** to help **YOU** through the process of receiving the promised products and services paid for + solutions for the multitude of financial dilemmas that came from dubious financial products that set investors up for financial ruin. And the much more that besets everyone everywhere in this changing 21st century global chaos society.

To be EMPOWERED, find out how the process begins by putting into action the tools in this book AND learn how to take CONTROL of YOUR life.

Read on...

HOW TO take CONTROL OF YOUR LIFE

Start the Empowerment Process

the HOW-TO

THIS is about the **PROCESS** of **making a list** of **what YOU** spend because **YOU** need to **determine how YOU use your income by listing all** the **ways YOU spend YOUR money**.
YOU are probably wondering what this budgeting process has to do with **EMPOWERMENT**—it's simple—**if YOU don't know where YOU spend your money YOU are helpless when there is 0 in the bank + 0 under the mattress at the end of the month. You are just as helpless to control your life even with plenty of disposable income when you can't spare a dime more for anything because there is never enough to cover whatever you spend.**
YET bills must be paid and there's so much more YOU can't afford but would like to have.

the Process

LOOK at your check book "RECORD KEEPER" + **ALL** the bank statements, make a **LIST** of everything **YOU** spend your money on. When you identify the "product" or "service" categories use this as YOUR diagram FOR how YOU DISTRIBUTE YOUR monthly income (see how I did it on page 19).

let's SUM up

SO FAR in this SECTION ONE you found out what EMPOWER means + HOW-TO take control of YOUR life. Also the way to Effect a Change in the manner you spend your money so you can enjoy more with your income.

but HOW???

Read on...

ACTION PLAN

the 3 category Lists

Your list is classified by what everyone **NEEDS** to have + what **YOU** know maintains **YOUR** friendships AND what would be nice to do as often as possible.

INCOME NET

ESSENTIALS	**SOCIAL**	**TIME OFF**
food	entertaining	vacations
mortgage (or rent)	dining out	
heating/cooling		
car		
health insurance/other		
banking-credit/debit cards		
cell phone and/or landline		
TV/cable or satellite		
Internet		
clothes/other purchases		
charity donations		
religious tithe		

It's clear—the column of ESSENTIALS is filled BUT fun time columns are much too short.

Read on...

YOU And Your Network

YOU AND YOUR NETWORK are connected by an ECONOMIC commonality NEED TO KNOW:

- **Government Grants that are available** for **Community + Neighborhood Organizations** to **explore beneficial solutions** to community **problems.**

- More about the Government **FOOD PROGRAM** called **SNAP** that was expanded **to higher income levels and now includes working families with children + the elderly over 75 years of age.**

- **Those** Heap **GOVERNMENT subsidized heating and air conditioning costs** which may fit **wage earners who are working but can't afford their energy cost,** as well as the **RETIRED whose income fits within the guidelines**.

more about Your Network

YOU AND YOUR NETWORK help each other in 3 ways: you have in common the economics of circumstances **bringing ALL of YOU together** to be **EMPOWERED to raise ONE loud VOICE** to effect a **CHANGE** in the way this 21st century of businesses and corporations offer their products and services to customers who want what they paid for.

PLUS

You AND Your Network can share the burden of finding the Local + State + Federal resources that CAN help each one of you receive the value you paid and contracted for.

PLUS

You AND your Network can BRAINSTORM about how to use your local, state & Federal government to achieve your goals + discover how YOU AND your NETWORK can find the answers to IMPORTANT QUESTIONS such as:

- **Are there any government grants or programs we are eligible to receive???**

one more thing

With a **"cooperation"** **NETWORK** of **HELPERS** to **SHARE** the **BURDEN** of researching government and other agencies to help resolve disputes with businesses on the **ESSENTIALS** list are **burdens divided up as follows:**
1. Pose a **"question"** re the above for the purpose of producing a list of websites on the computer screen to **"search engines"** like **GOOGLE** or **Yahoo"**—make note of the results in a word processing document produced for **NETWORK** distribution.
2. Have a scheduled NETWORK meeting and **divide up the compiled list of**

ARE YOU EMPOWERED??? Cynthia Lynn

"search engine" produced websites among those who have a computer, have volunteers to research "step 1" websites + others who put the useful information into a word processing document to **share** with one another at a **NETWORK "share" meeting**.

3. And get other members of the **NETWORK volunteer group** to **telephone** the **"help lines"** offered by **government agencies & consumer groups** to inquire about the **advise and mediate process for solving consumer issues.**

Read on...

ARE YOU EMPOWERED??? Cynthia Lynn

Federal Programs

The best source of information for Federal Programs is your CONGRESSIONAL REPRESENTATIVE. **In other countries there are the elected and sometimes appointed to levels of government.** In the USA your Board Of Elections has the name of the member who represents your district and in most cases will offer the telephone number. Keep in mind that in the USA your Congressional Representative has a STAFF MEMBER who SPECIALIZES in ferreting out government programs YOU or one of your friends might qualify for.

some popular USA Federal Programs

- The **FOOD program SNAP** has **expanded** to higher income levels **including working families with children** and **elderly over 75 years of age.**

- **"HEATING and AIR CONDITIONING"** cost is GOVERNMENT subsidized in some communities specifically FOR those wage earners who work but can't afford their energy cost AND Retired persons who qualify.

NOTES:
www.fns.usda.gov/snap/supplements is a Federal Government website informing about food benefits—if you aren't Computer

ARE YOU EMPOWERED??? Cynthia Lynn

savvy **find out** where to put the website address by using the "INDEX" to find the pages featuring **INTERNET TIPS**. The above mentioned government website "screen clipping is shown below":

Look at the far left of the website and SEE a list of options to pursue + apply for. ALSO discover about MORE USDA programs that are aimed at the consumer and explore PILOT programs that traditionally interest individuals with plenty of Disposable Income who want to be active in groups that seek to legislate for law change.
and more
See **SECTION THREE** for more "**ACTION FOR CHANGE**" suggestions with a "selection" of **www.thinkingoutloudan.blogspot.com**
2013 blogs that have been edited for this section.
+ more
Obtain information about government subsidies at **www.ehow.com/info_8623857**

ARE YOU EMPOWERED??? Cynthia Lynn

The previous "screen clipping" shows the name of this "ad sponsored" website. See the more detailed "screen clipping" below:

Grants for Replacement Air Conditioning

By Rod Howell, eHow Contributor . *last updated August 31, 2014*

The costs of replacing air conditioners in private homes, public housing units and commercial structures are covered by grants funded by several government agencies. Grants cover the removal of old or inoperable air conditioning systems and installation of new ones including labor expenses. Recipients can purchase

Read on...

YOUR Government Agencies
TIPS to keep in mind

When YOU are experiencing **problems** about products and services you paid for, remember that most **USA Federal and State Agencies** have **CONSUMER help lines to advise** about the ways to can take **ACTION** against **unscrupulous businesses and scams.**

AND

When you have **billing** + other issues with **"ESSENTIAL service" providers (electric, gas, landline telephone)** your **"City", "Town"** and **"County" governments** can **advise** about the **"wiring"** and **"grid" system of your neighborhood**. For example, **YOU** may find out from your local **"Building Department"** about **your** neighborhood's **"over-burdened electric grid,"** and the town/city Building Department may advise you about a solution: in this case about **"grid shut-off" switches** which need to be installed by the "service provider" + the Building Department Manager (or "Assistant") will also tell you which **"State Agency"** should be contacted for help to require the Electric service provider to do what is necessary to avoid power outages during inclement weather seasons.

AND

When you are having **billing** issues with your **"Internet"** or **"cellphone"** provider it's a good idea to contact the **"Federal agency"** that regulates these "services"**—see "SECTION TWO"** in this book **"TEST YOUR**

ARE YOU EMPOWERED??? Cynthia Lynn

KNOWLEDGE Questions + ANSWERS" under the topics "**Cell phone or landline,**" "**TV/cable or Satellite,**" also "**Internet,**" and find out if your state PSC regulates some provider services, you can also find out by looking for those topics in the **CONTENTS** of this book and the **INDEX**.

most importantly

Keep in mind that each **USA "City"** or "**Town**" **and/or** "**COUNTY**" allows the "**FRANCHISE**" of provider services for "**TV**" (cable and satellite) **+ "Internet"** in your area. **YOU can take ACTION** to insure that all the **INTERNET** and **TV CABLE/SATELLITE** providers in your area offer reasonably priced service.

AND

You can take ACTION—contact your **City Hall** to find out when the **Franchising Board** "**open to the Public**" meeting takes place so **YOU and YOUR NETWORK can attend to give input.** For instance, tell them **more competition for communication services is essential to keep prices down.**

You and your NETWORK can **communicate** with the **Federal agency** that **regulates all kinds of communication services: the FCC** (find Federal Communications Commission's website in the INDEX under websites). Use e-mail to give **your input** about what is lacking in **Federal Regulations** to protect consumers. It is important to let the agency bureaucrats know consumers are entitled to fairly priced Internet and TV Cable/satellite services, because these are **essential services** in a globally connected world.

Read on...

ARE YOU EMPOWERED???   Cynthia Lynn

the process of Change

In this 21st century of predator businesses that are not inclined to offer **essential services** and **products** for a **fair price,** the **ACTION PLAN for change** begins when **you identify YOUR economic category** and when you find out if paying for the **essentials** (listed on page 19 of this book) impacts the **quality of your social outings and vacation times.**

Did you know when it comes to **money YOU FIT** into **1** of **4 economic CATEGORIES???**

And did you know everyone is bound by **commonality** into **a NETWORK** that **reinforces our lives**, whether the **binding ties** be **religious/ethnic/same neighborhood.** Your **NETWORK** well could be anywhere **social activities take place**. OTHER kinds of **NETWORKS** have a **commonality** based on **friendships in a community**, or at the **work environment**.

In this mix of all **commonality** there is always a **particular shared economic situation** like those listed below:

- **There are 2 income categories STILL working—but 1 of the 2 is struggling to pay the bills**

  AND

- **RETIRED who thought they had enough to keep their WORKING LIFE STYLE**

  AND

- **RETIRED who have disposable income but are mired in the belief**

ARE YOU EMPOWERED??? Cynthia Lynn

it's NOT possible to TAKE ACTION because the opinions of peers don't accept the notion of EMPOWERMENT.

NOW to find **the income category you fit into:**

1. Do YOU fit into the "income category" of those who have plenty of disposable income BUT work hard to keep YOUR life style?

QUESTIONS

- **Am I** working too hard and let myself get cheated by businesses that don't give me what I pay for???

- **DO I** have to SLEEP LESS to fit in some free time to meet with friends???

- **Am I** STRESSED OUT by vacations BECAUSE I know I am MISSING OUT on what's happening at my job???

2. YOUR "income category" is working but struggling to pay the bills + sometimes no matter how hard you try YOU come up empty at the end of the month.

QUESTIONS

- **AM I** BROKE at the end of the month???

- **CAN I** afford to SOCIALIZE as much as I want???

- **CAN I** afford to VACATION???

3. YOU are in the "income category" of RETIRED who don't have enough money to maintain the WORKING LIFE STYLE.

QUESTIONS

- **AM I** UNHAPPY because my INCOME ISN'T ENOUGH for the ESSENTIALS I had when working + having to pinch pennies to get by at the end of the month???

- **CAN I** AFFORD TO SOCIALIZE whenever I want???

- **CAN I** afford to take the kind of VACATIONS that are special???

4. You are in the income category of RETIRED with plenty of disposable income AND **ANOTHER kind of problem:**

- **AM I** feeling old and without a purpose?

- **AM I** too old to be EMPOWERED???

- **CAN I** TAKE ACTION against sellers of products that CHEAT me out of what I paid for?

ARE YOU EMPOWERED???   Cynthia Lynn

Do you know that most of the products sold in this 21st century are made in 3rd world countries with no accountability to produce a good product because sellers of most products don't demand it?

let's sum up

So far you have found out that no matter what your income, **everyone is bound by their "income net."** And something is holding you from your potential when **your "income net" constricts the way you enjoy your life**. As well this is true even when you have plenty of money, because you **lack time TO BE EMPOWERED TO TAKE ACTION to make lifestyle changes.**

and

the **process of CHANGE** takes place when **you walk the path to becoming EMPOWERED** to **get control of your life**.

and

you are **LEARNING** what **you can do** to NOT BE **CHEATED by predator businesses** that take more than their share of **your money** for a **service and/or product** that **you paid for + HOW-TO TAKE ACTION** when these businesses **AVOID GIVING YOU WHAT YOU PAID FOR**.

Read on...

SECTION TWO

POINTERS plus HOW-TO

and
**TEST your knowledge
QUESTIONS and Answers**

ARE YOU EMPOWERED???   Cynthia Lynn

POINTERS plus HOW-TO

At some time or another **YOU** are subject to people in power positions that answer the phones who prefer not to tell **you** what **you** need to know about **your** mortgage, credit/debit cards, cable TV, telephone, bank account + they aren't interested in performing above their job level.

OR perhaps they aren't well trained and feel threatened when **you** ask to speak to the supervisor. **They say you are "out of order" and "abusive."**

YOUR Government Agencies

YOU are **EMPOWERED** when **you** know that **HELP** is available from **your** "**Government**." It's up to **YOU** to call **your** **local City/Town Hall** AND **ask** questions to determine which **Department** knows about the **essential provider "services"** offered to **your** AREA and Neighborhood, You are walking the **EMPOWERED** path when you find out if someone in that **Department** can offer some helpful information.

YOUR Federal and State governments have Departments and Agencies that are **goldmines of information for CONSUMERS** like you. Those who feel cheated by a "business" or "service" that doesn't give **you** what you pay for, and those who want to know what they are entitled to receive.

more
"**Government**" **uses your TAX DOLLARS** to create an Agency with Department aimed at

showing voters "Government" is there to attend to the public need.

and

"Government" employs taxpayers to do the job of protecting the public against scams + predator businesses that cheat customers.

and

"GOVERNMENT" has created Agencies that have specialized "Departments" to control and supervise businesses that need supervising—like, Licensing of Trucking, Rail and Freight Carriers, categories of Telecommunications, Radio/TV Broadcasting stations, and so on. Even **your** hair dresser and/or barber needs a LICENSE issued by "Government."

and

"Government" makes money every time a **license is needed** to **work** and/or do **business.**

Read on...

ARE YOU EMPOWERED??? Cynthia Lynn

I N T E R N E T TIPS

more about your Network

Your NETWORK can ease the burden of finding information to benefit all. Those who can access a computer don't have to be computer savvy because the **"Internet Tips"** offered in this book give the **"how-to"** information. Not everyone is computer savvy knowledgeable when it comes to using a "search engine" to its full capacity, and for anyone who finds it difficult, there is an easy method to find the specific websites listed in this book.

DO THE FOLLOWING:

1. "www" starts the website listing.
2. Place the website name in the search engine's **"search"** slot (always in the middle of the search engine webpage).
3. Don't use the possible "suggestions," instead pick the correct website among all the listings that appear when you use the **"search"** slot.
<u>**NOTE**</u>:
In this book to help the reader identify the correct website a reduced size **"screen clipping"** of the correct web page is shown immediately after the website listing.

for the computer savvy

The **"Internet Tips"** listed below are aimed at insuring accuracy without time-consuming list searches because often the

ARE YOU EMPOWERED??? Cynthia Lynn

search engine **"search slot"** has listings similar to the specific website mentioned and IT'S NECESSARY TO CHECK OUT ALL THE LISTINGS TO FIND the right one.

1. **"Copy"** each **"web address"** that you find in this book to place in the slot for the **"web address"** of **your search engine "home page"** and begin the "web address" with "http://."

but first

2. Use the **"mouse"** to highlight the **"search engine home page address."**

then

3. Use the "**keyboard shortcut**" "**Ctrl +X**" and again use the **"mouse"** to place the more accurate **"web address"** you copied into the blank space of the **"search engine home page address."**

and

4. In the "**search engine home page address**" which is still a blank space key in "**http://**" to add to the "**www "web address** I listed in this book.

FIND OUT
how-to
INTERNET TOPIC SEARCH

1. Use the **"search slot"** of **your "search engine home page"** to ask a question.

2. Begin the question with **"how to..."**

3. Add the **"topic key word"** of each **specific topic** you need.

4. From the list of websites that appear **investigate** the ones that seem most promising

AND

All of the above is listed in the **Contents SECTION TWO** under "**INTERNET TIPS**" + these pages are listed in the **INDEX** under the topic you need.

Read on...

ARE YOU EMPOWERED???   Cynthia Lynn

"Consumer Advocates"

Someone you may or may not have heard of is the granddaddy of advocate activist "consumerism"—it's **RALPH NADER**, and he came galloping into the national scene in 1965. This was when the manufacture of automobiles was focused on speed and designs of cars which put drivers into life threatening vehicles, and created hazards when traveling on the newly built 3 and 4 lane Interstate highways of America. The nation's newspapers featured stories about so many highway deaths that Congress held hearings aimed at questioning auto makers like GM and Ford about the large number of fatalities hoping to determine what was wrong. During that time of Congressional car safety hearings, the book *UNSAFE AT ANY SPEED* was written by Ralph Nader and became a best seller.

What Ralph Nader revealed brought about **DOT** (Department of Transportation) regulations to oversee car manufacturers who sell their product in the USA to make them adhere to mandated safety considerations + apply consumer crash test ratings of their product to make available for the public to see.

Now **car safety is the main function of** the Federal government's **DOT** agency, also the Director of that agency is a member of the President's cabinet.

On the next page see the "screen clipping" of website: **www.dot.gov**:

ARE YOU EMPOWERED??? Cynthia Lynn

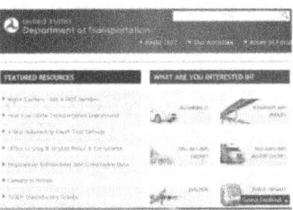

NOTES:

All of the Federal departments **www.dot.gov** supervises were created to protect the public from "predator businesses" engaged in one of the many forms of "transportation." On the **DOT website** see the **list** below and use the links to find tollfree phone numbers for help from a **DOT** "consumer advocate" trained to advise about government mediated solutions:

    FAA aviation
    FHWA roadways and bridges
    FMCSA trucking and motor coaches
    FRA railways
    FTA public transport
    MARAD maritime
    NHTSA automobiles
    OIG Inspector general
    OST Office of the Secretary
    PHMSA pipelines and HazMat
    RITA research
    SLSDC St. Lawrence Seaway
    STB surface transportation

ALL OF THE ABOVE are government departments that can help when a business engaged in transportation "**refuses to compensate you for YOUR loss**."

Read on...

ARE YOU EMPOWERED??? Cynthia Lynn

Consumer Friendly FED

www.usa.gov/directory/consumerorgs is a Federal website dedicated to **Consumer Organizations**. Use the topic organized **A to Z website listings** for consumer organized groups that provide free advice about the right government agency **to help with the problem.** See the "screen clipping" below:

Services and Information + Government Agencies and elected officials are located at the top of the website, and the link **CONTACT US** located at the upper left side triggers the **phone number**.

<u>**NOTES**</u>:

Consumer organizations will recommend seeking advice from Federal or State Government Agency Departments, but keep in mind that more **"Consumer"** help can be accessed by calling your County, or Local Governments.

There are also **"Consumer Organizations"** dedicated to advocate for consumer issues with Government to **affect a change in the status quo**. One of those organizations is: **www.citizen.org/Page**. See the "screen clipping" on the next page**:**

ARE YOU EMPOWERED???   **Cynthia Lynn**

Use the "**contact us**" link for the list of phone numbers + e-mail addresses of staffers who work in policy areas. They will advise groups like **you and your network** how-to advocate with your state and local governments for more consumer protection against predator businesses and service providers who refuse to acknowledge overcharges + won't provide a **complaint process mediated solution**.

Read on...

ARE YOU EMPOWERED??? Cynthia Lynn

Another Suggestion

I used a search engine for a **"topical search"** and entered into the blank slot the **"KEY"** word **"consumer advocates"**
and
I found the website **www.naca.net** See the "screen clipping" below:

NOTES:
Some of the **NACA attorneys** might already be handling issues that **you** and **your Network** have with predator businesses that seek to cheat customers out of the "products" and "services" paid for, as well, these are lawyers who prosecute **"class action" lawsuits and** typically work on a **"percentage" case basis**, which means the law firm pays for all costs in exchange for a **"percentage" of the compensation** if the case is won.

Read on...

The Sum Up

You and your Network are cooperating for the purpose of obtaining information about the many laws and regulations the US Congress created to protect consumers who feel **cheated out of the "service"** or **"product"** they paid for.

and

You with **your Network can become "computer savvy"** to find **"clues"** on the **"Internet"**.

and more

The connection to your highway of knowledge is the **internet search engine**.

with another +

"Topical search" QUESTIONS sources provide the **websites** for **Government** + for **Consumer group sources** that **either YOU** or someone in **YOUR NETWORK** has to **contact** for advice about the **specific issue** causing the **problem**.

Read on...

TEST your knowledge QUESTIONS and Answers

Why's and Wherefores about TEST Your Knowledge

In this **SECTION TWO** **"TEST your knowledge QUESTIONS"** are based on the **"ESSENTIALS"** LIST from page 19 of this book. The **answers** provide suggestions with **websites** to **access** + telephone numbers to **Federal** and **State government agencies you** may not know exist just a phone call away for US citizens who need advice about **TAKING ACTION** about **predator businesses/sellers of products** that aren't **providing the service and/or product paid for**. The **answers** to the **TEST your knowledge QUESTIONS also** give information about how to **access** certain **"ad sponsored websites"** that offer excellent suggestions about **consumer activist groups** + **expert advice with practical solutions**.

Schedule a Network Meeting

Periodically inform members what has been learned after research based on the **"ESSENTIALS"** LIST of page 19 of this book. It's a good idea to schedule monthly and/or

ARE YOU EMPOWERED???　　　　　Cynthia Lynn

weekly **NETWORK** meetings to exchange information about specific **Internet websites** that reference **TOPIC questions** Remember, if everyone takes a turn at the research chores this eases the burden of collecting information for the benefit of all and puts one and all on the **path to becoming EMPOWERED**.

more re QUESTIONS and Answers

Keep in mind many of the exampled websites change the look of their site and the "screen clippings" shown in this book may be different than what you see on the computer screen. Iin that case, use the **search slot** of the **search engine** and key in **"www"** with the name of the website to find the correct updated site.

Read on...

ARE YOU EMPOWERED???   Cynthia Lynn

TOPIC: 1. food
QUESTION A
I'm part of a household that is not earning enough to pay those ever rising food prices. Where can I find out if I am eligible for government help?
Answer
The US Department of Agriculture determines the eligibility for the **"SNAP"** (supplemental nutritional assistance program) find information at **www.fns.usda.gov/snap/eligibility** See "screen clipping" below:

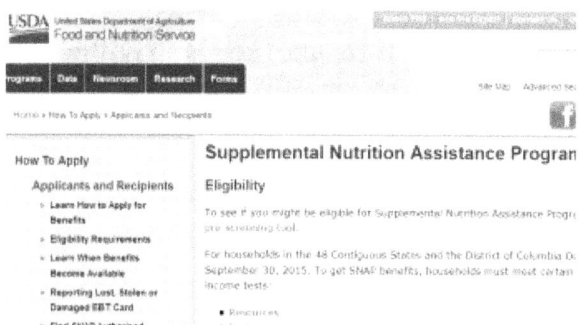

READ the "Resources" guidelines and scroll down to see the income eligibility list. To submit an online application link to **www.snap-help.com** See "screen clipping" below:

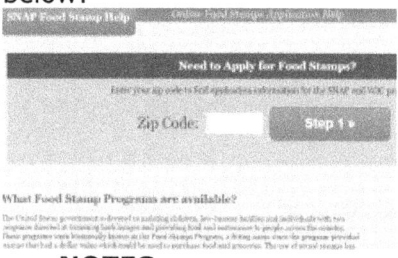

NOTES:
You can also contact your local "City Hall" and "County" to find out if they have a low

ARE YOU EMPOWERED??? Cynthia Lynn

income assistance program. This may include distribution of farm produce at reduced rates **OR** a locally subsidized "food pantry."

Often religious organizations administrate a "Community Food Service" program. Ask at any place of religious observance whether they know of any "food pantries" in your community. Find out if there are "Farms" in your local area and either "call or visit" to ask if they might be willing to offer you and your **NETWORK** some produce at a reduced rate.

ARE YOU EMPOWERED??? Cynthia Lynn

TOPIC: 1. food/continued...
QUESTION B
Are there community sponsored food groups that sponsor farmer coops for those who are not able to spend what it costs to buy fresh vegetables? Where can I find out about it?
Answer
Information about state funded food programs are on the Federal government website: **www.fns.usda.gov/cacfp** See **"How To Apply"** on the right under the top link with more links underneath. See "screen clipping" below:

more on this topic
NOTE:

I posed this QUESTION to the Internet "search engine": **"Community Food Programs"** AND I came up with a LIST of websites, many of which were about programs in states that are funding in communities nationwide. One website was **www.farmaid.org/site** See "screen clipping" on the next page:

ARE YOU EMPOWERED???   **Cynthia Lynn**

FUNDING OPPORTUNITIES

MAKING THE CASE

SOURCES

Family Farmers and Economic Opportunities

WHEN you LINK to the above WEBSITE you'll find out about Federal/State government "aid grants." Use this information to get your community ACCESS TO FRESH FOOD.

TOPIC: 2. monthly mortgage (or rent)

QUESTION A

I notice that my monthly mortgage payment goes up every year, and when I asked why, I was told that the escrow payment went up because the **PMI** (PRIVATE MORTGAGE INSURANCE) rate goes up every year + so does the homeowners insurance.

What can I do to get my own mortgage insurance?

Answer

www.bankrate.com/the-basics-of-private-mortgage-insurance is a "public access website" that explains the process of obtaining **PMI** This site is on the list of websites that come up in the list populated by "**search engines**" websites about **PMI** See screen clipping below:

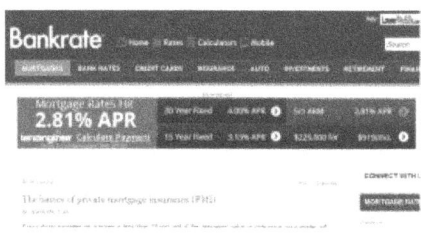

NOTES:

Once you find out about **PMI**, you'll need to use the Internet again to access this website: **www.helpwithmybank.gov** See "screen clipping" on the next page:

ARE YOU EMPOWERED??? Cynthia Lynn

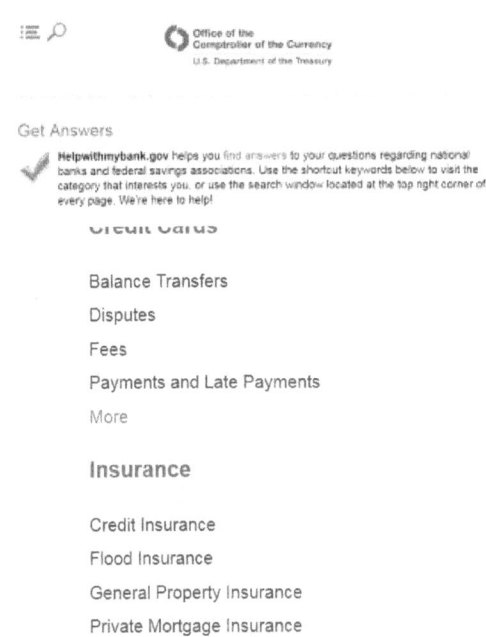

NOTES: (continued)
At the above website scroll down further to find the link to "Insurance" and scroll to the bottom of the website, look on the right. Below the link "**more**" brings up another part of this website, the **tollfree customer assistance links.** See "screen clipping" on the next page:

NOTES: (continued)

Re **PMI** if you have a VA loan and haven't put the 20% down payment find the website **www.helpwithmybank.gov**. Their Consumer Assistance help line offers other options, like planning ahead to get what is needed to lower that high mortgage payment.

ARE YOU EMPOWERED???   Cynthia Lynn

TOPIC: 2. monthly mortgage (or rent) continued...

QUESTION B.
I pay my monthly rent promptly, but my landlord doesn't fix the broken appliances unless I call several times, and even then I have to wait several weeks sometimes.

I've had emergency maintenance problems and there is no response to my telephone call, plus I've had to call an hourly 24 hour maintenance service and pay the bill myself. When I wanted to be reimbursed I was told that I didn't wait until I received a call back, so I am not entitled to it.

What can I do? Is there someone I could complain to?

Answer

I posed the question: **do states help with tenant landlord issues** and on the search engine list of websites, I found **www.ehow.com/issues-landlords** See "screen clipping" below:

NOTES:
Call your "local" City Hall" because usually the **Building Department** knows about

ARE YOU EMPOWERED??? Cynthia Lynn

regulations for the **maintenance of apartments**. If your "Town" is run by a "Board of Commissioners" call the "City Clerk" at the "City Hall" to ask for the **Building Department**. Some cities and towns have **renters associations**. Find out if there is one in your area with your "**search engine's search slot.**" Use the topic "**renters association**" and don't forget to add the **Town, City or County where you are located**.

more

When maintenance issues could affect your family's health call **the State, County and City/Town health departments.** Ask if there are **health regulations for apartment maintenance problems affecting the family's health**. It could be that your plumbing maintenance problem has brought mold into your apartment which is recognized as a health hazard.

ARE YOU EMPOWERED???   **Cynthia Lynn**

TOPIC: 2. monthly mortgage (or rent) continued...
QUESTION C

I went to a local bank to get a mortgage because I like the staff and I want someone I know to call if there is a problem and now my mortgage has been sold to a large bank in another state and the service is terrible.

Can I refinance at a local bank that will not sell my mortgage and also get a better deal? I've had my mortgage for 5 years and all my payments are on time.

Answer

www.helpwithmybank.gov/get-answers/mortgages/index is a helpful website. See "screen clipping" below:

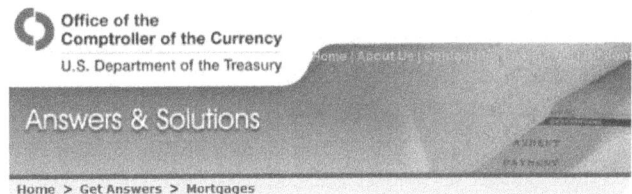

ARE YOU EMPOWERED???   Cynthia Lynn

Use your mouse to access the "**General Mortgage Questions**" link to find the answer to the question. See "screen clipping" below:

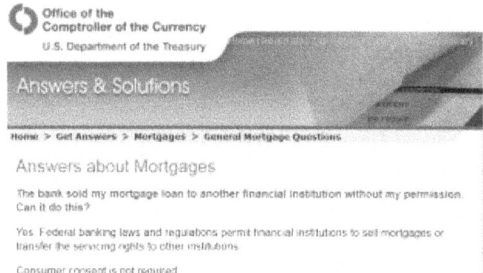

The tollfree Consumer Assistance for information + more advice is on the far lower left.

NOTES:

Keep in mind that you need to ask for a "**NO TRANSFER clause**" **refinanced mortgage loan**. Your problem is finding a bank willing to give a "**refinanced loan**" with "**no transfer clause.**"

more

The **mortgage industry** is mostly **non-Federally regulated** but your **State Banking Department** may suggest a reliable bank to query. Find the website **www.csbs.org** to locate the "Banking Department" in your State. See "screen clipping" below:

and www.usa.gov/directory/consumerorgs lets you check out consumer groups to belong to if you chose to **advocate for change** +

ARE YOU EMPOWERED???   Cynthia Lynn

participate in a **"consumer group lobby umbrella."** See "screen clipping" below:

These groups regularly speak to Congressional representatives of both political parties. Use the vetted list links to find the category "mortgage industry" to pick one. Let them tell you how and when to participate in "e-mail" and "telephone" campaigns the group sets up to accomplish group goals.

AND MORE
Seeking solutions means **YOU** and **your NETWORK are EMPOWERED** to start a **petition drive** in your community for a **"60 day notification to the mortgagee in the event of a mortgage sale to another BANK."** It's always good to add this: **"the community seeks compromise legislation,"** and send the petition to your Federal + State representatives.

and
Keep in mind **"government compromise" gets law proposed and passed.**

ARE YOU EMPOWERED??? Cynthia Lynn

TOPIC: 2. monthly mortgage (or rent) continued...

QUESTION D

I'd like to live in a house instead of an apartment, but I have no money to use as a down payment though what I pay in apartment rent would pay for a mortgage.

Is there a way for someone like me to have my own home?

Answer

www.hud.gov.portal/topics/buying_a_home See "screen clipping" below":

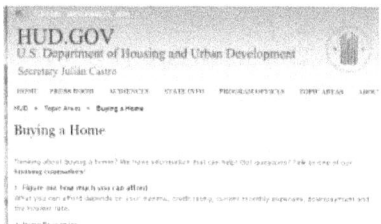

this is a Federal government website with a **Fed solution** to this **QUESTION D** dilemma. To find your state HUD information look for **"STATE INFO"** and SCROLL down to "topic areas" for the 2 items that apply to owning a home with Federal help. See "screen clipping" on the following page:

ARE YOU EMPOWERED??? Cynthia Lynn

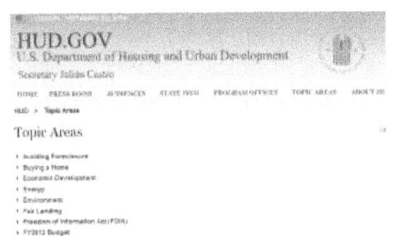

The 2 topics that suggest ways to own your own home are: "**Houses for Sale**" and "**HUD Homes**."
NOTE:
As I've mentioned numerous times it's your "Government" and they want to help. Think of it as help in exchange. **YOU pay taxes** and **"Government"** offers **solutions**.
MORE
When seeking out what you need YOU ARE EMPOWERED.

TOPIC: 2. monthly mortgage (or rent) continued...

QUESTION E
I live in an apartment but I've noticed that each year the rent rises by more than $20. Can they raise my rent as high as they want?

Is there any limit on how much rents can go up for renters who have the same apartment up for lease renewal?

Answer
www ehow.com/info_ 7852265 is an "ad sponsored" website that offers some good advice. See "screen clipping" below:

www.hud.gov rental assistance website gives information about the guidelines for qualifying. See "screen clipping" below:

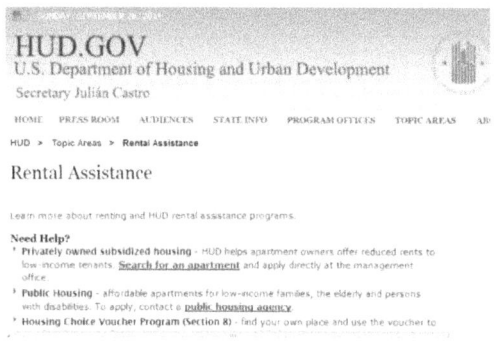

ARE YOU EMPOWERED???   Cynthia Lynn

NOTES:
It's always a good idea to use 2 search engines when **POSING A QUESTION.** For instance about this question: **"Landlord/tenant issues"** I used **Yahoo** without any good result but I tried **GOOGLE** and found the website **www.nolo.com legal encyclopedia renters rights** Screen clipping" below:

Scroll down to the lower portion of this website for **"Law Blogs."** See "screen-clipping" below:

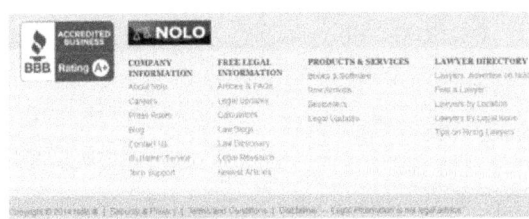

Under "Law Blogs". is another website. See "screen clipping" below:

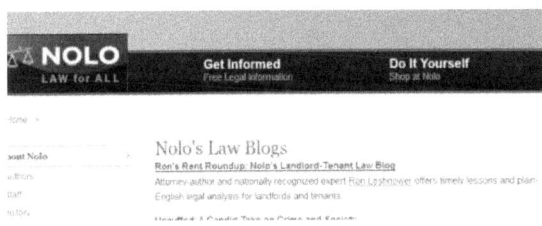

ARE YOU EMPOWERED???   Cynthia Lynn

At the top on the list of "**Nolo's Law Blogs**" is an expert who may know more information about the answer to this question.

more

Be **EMPOWERED** when you **pose a question** to both **Yahoo and Google search engines** to **SEE** if there's another website on the list for **TOPIC 1. ANSWER E** to research and share with your **network**.

ARE YOU EMPOWERED???   Cynthia Lynn

TOPIC: 3. heating/cooling

QUESTION A
We've had several short power outages not caused by bad weather that have effected my electronic devices, and I have surge protection for them, but the frequency (sometimes 2 or 3 in 1 hour) has caused my computer and printer to stop working.

My devices are just 2 years old and I had no problems before the outages became so frequent in the same day. I complained to my electric provider, but they said they aren't responsible for accidents or other problems affecting the electric grid. How can I get reimbursed for the cost of my ruined devices?

Answer
www.wikipedia.org/wiki/Public_utilities_commission website offers an overview + more. See screen clipping below:

WIKIPEDIA
The Free Encyclopedia

Public utilities commission

From Wikipedia, the free encyclopedia

A utilities commission, utility regulatory commission (URC), public governing body that regulates the rates and services of a public utility. I may be civil service oversight bodies, rather than utilities regulators.

The utility that is being regulated may be owned by the consumers that may be a stockholder owned utility either publicly traded on a stock exc

They are able to operate because of legal monopolies, which means th

Countries:

- Anguilla Public Utilities Commission
- Bahamas Public Utilities Commission [1]
- Belize Public Utilities Commission [2]
- Public Utilities Commission of Sri Lanka [3]
- Superintendencia de Servicios Sanitarios de Chile [4]
- Commission de Regulation de l'Energie [5]

To find the list of USA Public Service Commissions scroll down o the lower portion of this website. See next page "screen clipping":

ARE YOU EMPOWERED??? Cynthia Lynn

United States:
- Alabama Public Service Commission [6]
- Regulatory Commission of Alaska [7]
- Arizona Corporation Commission [8]
- Arkansas Public Service Commission [9]
- California Public Utilities Commission [10]
- Colorado Public Utilities Commission [11]
- Connecticut Department of Public Utility Control [12]
- Delaware Public Service Commission [13]
- District of Columbia Public Service Commission [14]
- Florida Public Service Commission [15]
- Georgia Public Service Commission [16]
- Hawaii Public Utilities Commission [17]
- Idaho Public Utilities Commission [18]

When you find your state's website call to ASK how you can receive reimbursement for your loss.

NOTES:

The **Public Service Commission** is a mediating authority. Before you call make sure that you have proof of purchase for your ruined electronics and be ready to give your **PSC** the amount you will accept commensurate with the number of years you have owned those electronics. This is necessary for the mediation process to commence and for you to achieve a monetary resolution (usually a compromise $ amount).

more

Another "Government" source is your **Local government** website. Put the name in the "search slot" of your search engine, find the telephone number of the **BUILDING DEPARTMENT**, and ask about local government problems with the frequent outages in your neighborhood + inquire about construction complaints against the utility provider. You can use that information to prop up your claim with your **PSC** for reimbursement.

ARE YOU EMPOWERED???   Cynthia Lynn

TOPIC: 3. heating/cooling
continued...

QUESTION B
The electric rates have been going up to the point that I have to avoid heating some rooms in my house. I have young children and they now are frequently sick with colds. In the summer, I have to cut off the air conditioning to avoid the cost. But then I've noticed that fans are also raising my electric bill. Are the electric companies allowed to raise the rates as often as they want?

Am I eligible for help if I am having trouble paying?

Answer
www.wikipedia.org/wiki/public_utilities_commission (as in ANSWER to QUESTION A) has a list of state **PSCs** where you can access the **PSC** tollfree phone number. Ask their trained specialists how you can weigh in when your Public Utility wants to raise the electric rates. Also ask how often the rates can be raised. Each state has rules and regulations in place for Public Utilities when asking for rate changes.

In answer to your question about subsidies information the website that comes up at the top of the Yahoo search engine list will help.: **www.acf.hhs.gov/programs/ocs/liheap**
Screen clipping below:

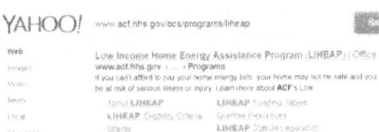

ARE YOU EMPOWERED???   **Cynthia Lynn**

Use your mouse to access any of the 6 topics. To find out whether you qualify scroll down to **"Eligibility criteria."** See "screen clipping" below:

The website's guidelines will show for the current year, scroll down to find out.

ARE YOU EMPOWERED???   Cynthia Lynn

TOPIC 3. Heating/cooling
continued...
QUESTION C
Are the electric companies regulated? If so, who regulates what they charge customers? Do they need an approval to add surcharges?

Answer
wikipedia.org/wiki/Public_utilities_commission
as in Answers A and B offers a link to your state's **PSC** website to ask about utility "surcharges" that impact you and your NETWORK.
> **NOTE**:
> **www.consumeraffairs.com/news04/2012/06/utility-surcharges-fees** has the article written by Truman Lewis staff writer for "*Consumer Affairs*" with the details about the 2012 consumer alert notice. See "screen clipping" below:

Read this online article which details how the AARP does advocate for the consumer. Call the AARP in your state, and access **www.usa.gov/directory/consumerorgs**, find the "screen clipping" below on next page:

ARE YOU EMPOWERED???   Cynthia Lynn

This is the Federal government website where you can locate a "CONSUMER GROUP" in your state activating against Utilities using loopholes in the law regulating Public Utilities.

and

now you are on the PATH to becoming EMPOWERED...

ARE YOU EMPOWERED??? Cynthia Lynn

TOPIC: 3. heating/cooling
continued...

QUESTION D
I think that I am being overcharged for electricity. My electric meter is more than 10 years old and has never been changed or calibrated.

When I asked my electric company to check it, they told me all the meters are made to last for 20 years or more. Also they said meters don't need to be recalibrated. Who can help me with my problem?

Answer
Call your "utility provider" to ask once more for a new electric meter and log your call with **"TIME and DATE+ Customer Service agent first NAME/last name initial and the CALL CENTER LOCATION."** If the answer is still negative ask for the agent's supervisor and log **"first name with last name initial."** At **www.Wikipedia.org/wiki/public_utilities_ commission** Locate your **PSC** to present information about your call to the Utility and ask for help to resolve this issue.

TOPIC: 4. commute

QUESTION A
Who regulates the charge for my driver's license and car plate?

Is there a way to lower my cost?

Answer
NCSL.org. is non-profit and non-partisan: **www.ncsl.org/research/transportation/registration-and-title-fees-by-state** shows all DMV departments by state with title fees + registration fees. See "screen clipping" below:

Call your **DMV** to inquire if your license and plates cost less if you appear in person + find out about a license plate that cost the least of the others offered by your state **DMV**.
> **NOTE**:
> Wikipedia's website has a historic overview + link to your state **DMV** website:

ARE YOU EMPOWERED???   Cynthia Lynn

wikipedia.org/wiki/Department_of_Motor_Vehicles, see "screen clipping" below:

United States [edit]

The Uniform Vehicle Code prefers the name "Department of Motor Vehicles".[1] The acronym "DMV" is most commonly used to describe the agency (where it exists); however, diverse titles are used in different jurisdictions. Unless otherwise indicated below, one agency or division regulates driver licensing, vehicle registration, and vehicle titles.

State/Territory	Agency responsible for driver licensing and vehicle title and registration	Parent agency Supplementary notes
Alabama	Driver License Division (driver licensing) and Motor Vehicle Division (vehicle registration and title)	The Driver License Division is a division of the Alabama Department of Public Safety, whereas Motor Vehicle Division is a division of the Alabama Department of Revenue.
Alaska	Division of Motor	Division of the Alaska Department of Administration; previously under the Alaska

ARE YOU EMPOWERED???   Cynthia Lynn

TOPIC: 4. commute/continued...

QUESTION B
I have parking fees to pay in order to park my car where I work. Is there a way to save some money?

Answer
Your employer can claim a tax write off to refund your expense. Search for the website **www.wikipedia.org/wiki/Employer_transportation_benefits_in_the_United_States**. See "screen clipping" below:

Speak to your employer re a petty cash reimbursement for your parking expenses **OR** you have the option to claim your parking fees on your Federal and State taxes if you itemize. Ask your tax preparer.
NOTE:
There should be **Public transportation** to get you where you need to go and communities that want jobs in their area provide it. If no

ARE YOU EMPOWERED???   Cynthia Lynn

convenient bus or train stop exists in your area contact your Local and County government to ask for a **public transportation** stop in your neighborhood. If there isn't any public transport where you work **TAKE ACTION**. Ask your employer to ask the **"transportation authority"** about adding a stop to a route that bisects or crosses within walking distance of the company.

and
whenever YOU TAKE ACTION you are EMPOWERED.

ARE YOU EMPOWERED???   Cynthia Lynn

TOPIC 4. commute/continued...
QUESTION C

I use a commuter train to get to work and I have to pay to park in the train parking lot.

Who regulates the fees? Is there a way to save some money?

Answer
See the **Answer** to **QUESTION B** and call your local government City Hall to inquire about the assessment of "parking lot fees" at the commuter rail station. Ask about attending a scheduled City meeting for **"parking lot assessments."** Also inquire about **income qualified residence permits** + other ways to lower the train parking lot fee.

NOTES:

Keep in mind that **taking ACTION** requires a little time and patience to ferret out what you need to know, but the result is well worth it

and

taking ACTION means you can manage your money.

ARE YOU EMPOWERED??? Cynthia Lynn

TOPIC: 4 commute/continued...

QUESTION D
Is there a regulatory agency that regulates train fares? If so, would they have information about ways to lower my fare?

Answer

Search for the website **www.dot.gov/contact-us).** This is the Federal regulatory agency for all forms of Public Transportation. See "screen clipping" below:

Use the customer service telephone number at the website top center. Ask them who regulates your train service.

more
Search for the website **www.Wikipedia.org/wiki/Department_of_Transportation** This is the best website for an overview of US Transportation Departments + links to your state's website. See next page "screen clipping":

ARE YOU EMPOWERED??? Cynthia Lynn

Article Talk   Read Edit View history Search

Department of Transportation

6 External links

List of U.S. state and insular area departments of
[edit]

- Alabama Department of Transportation (**ALDOT**)
- Alaska Department of Transportation and Public Facilities (**DOT&PF**)
- Arizona Department of Transportation (**ADOT**)
- Arkansas State Highway and Transportation Department (**AHTD**)
- California Department of Transportation (**Caltrans**)
- Colorado Department of Transportation (**CDOT**)

Call the **Customer Assistance** number to ask about your commuter rail line + who to call to find out about the various commuter fares that you may qualify for. For example, if you are a **Senior** you may have a special fare.

ARE YOU EMPOWERED???   Cynthia Lynn

TOPIC: 4. commute/continued...

QUESTION E

What Federal and/or state agencies are in charge of the Interstate highway system? Is there a State/Federal plan to help motorists carpool? Where can I find out about it?

Answer

www.fhwa.gov/congestion/state_information has the information you need, but that doesn't mean your state is actively pursuing car pooling in special lanes or special lanes at toll centers. See the website "screen clipping" below:

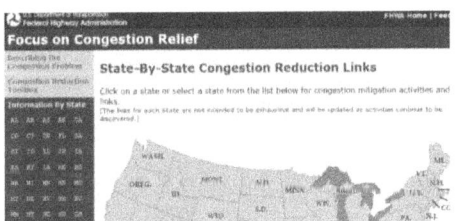

Scroll down and find another link. See "screen clipping" below:

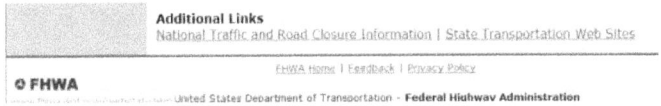

Call your state's Consumer Assistance telephone number to find out about your state car pool sharing programs.

NOTES:
If your state doesn't have a car pool sharing program ask your employer about

ARE YOU EMPOWERED???   Cynthia Lynn

putting up a flyer on the company employee bulletin board to locate willing participants living near your community. Give a suggested lunch meeting date to work out the arrangement for a car pooling schedule.

AND query your neighbors within a 2 mile vicinity at nearby apartment complexes + housing developments for willing car-pool participants who might be working in the vicinity of your place of employment.

more

All of the above means YOU are EMPOWERED to TAKE ACTION to "effect a change" about how you manage your money...

ARE YOU EMPOWERED??? Cynthia Lynn

TOPIC: 5. health insurance/other
QUESTION A
My homeowners insurance goes up every year and my insurance agent says there's a built in percentage for the estimated cost of replacement which goes up every year.

Is the insurance industry regulated? I don't live in a flood prone area, and I am not in an area subject to extreme weather hazards. Are there other ways for me to lower my homeowners insurance?

Answer
www.helpwithmybank.gov is a Federal government website that will help you with your questions. See screen clipping below:

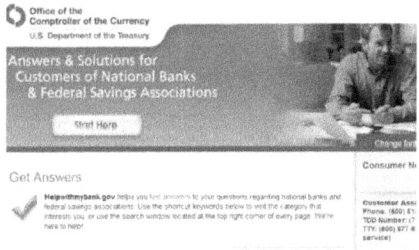

Call the **Customer Assistance** tollfree telephone on the right of the website under the heading **Consumer News** for answers to your question.
> **NOTE**:
> **www.naic.org/state_web_map** allows you to find your state's insurance department. See "screen clipping" next page:

ARE YOU EMPOWERED???   Cynthia Lynn

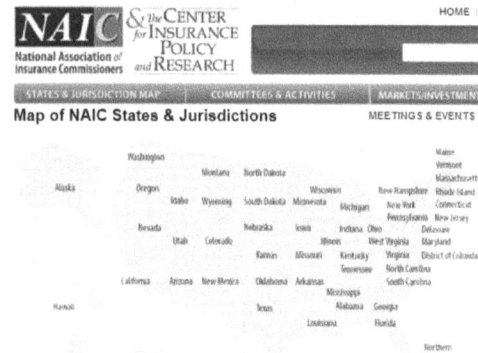

At your state's Insurance Department website locate the **consumer Information contact phone** to inquire about state regulations for your property insurance. Also ask about ways to lower your insurance charges.

TOPIC: 5. health insurance/other insurance–continued...

QUESTION B
My car insurance is getting very high, and when I asked my insurance agent if I could lower it, he tells me that I need what I have.

Where can I find out about what is required and what is not?

Answer
www.naic.org/state_web_map (as in ANSWER to QUESTION A) offers state Department of Insurance websites (or whatever Department may regulate your state's insurance offerings). Find the **consumer assistance** contact phone number and inquire to determine whether your current insurance can be lowered.

NOTES:

www.personalinsure.about.com/od/auto is sponsored by insurance companies and offers some interesting information that may help answer more about how to lower your car insurance. See "screen clipping" next page:

ARE YOU EMPOWERED??? Cynthia Lynn

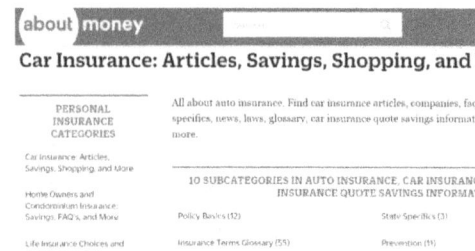

Keep in mind that that the amount of driving you do has an influence on your choice of insurance. If you are ever involved in a car crash with severe injuries to passengers your car insurance may not keep you from the possibility of your assets being seized to pay some portion not covered by your vehicle protection.

Ask your lawyer about protecting your assets from a lawsuit that seeks more than your vehicle protection.

ARE YOU EMPOWERED???   Cynthia Lynn

TOPIC: 5. health insurance/other insurance–continued...

QUESTION C
I worry that my children won't have a caregiver if I die, but the cost of life insurance is too high for what I approximate they will need.

What I'm looking for is for some unbiased advice about alternatives. Is the insurance industry regulated and would the government regulation authority know where I can get the information I need?

Answer
www.ehow.com/about_5326702_term-vs-whole-life-insurance an "ad-sponsored" website offers expert information to answer some aspects of your question. See "screen clipping" below:

This website explores the pros and the cons of what may be the best affordable insurance for your family. When you consult your insurance broker about **TERM INSURANCE** and **LIFE INSURANCE** you will then have in mind which of the two is best for you.

ARE YOU EMPOWERED??? Cynthia Lynn

TOPIC: 5. health insurance/other insurance-continued...

QUESTION D

I'm not getting the benefits that are listed in my health insurance plan handbook. I called and each time I'm told by the customer service they have to research my complaint. Is there anyone I can complain to?

Answer

www.attys.org/us-attorney-generals is the Federal website with links to your state's ATTORNEY GENERAL. See "screen clipping" below:

Call your **AG's consumer help** phone number to inquire if they have a **health care hotline** that may help resolve your issue. Ask if there is another department in your state that handles health insurance issues.

NOTE:

www.naic.org/state_web_map is the website that offers a link to your state's Insurance Department (or whatever state Department) is charged with insurance regulatory authority. Notify them that your health insurance company isn't resolving your issue—the regulatory authority in your state will advise the company + insist that your issue be resolved. Usually the company's **license to do business** as a health insurance provider in your state is an incentive.

TOPIC: 5. health insurance/other insurance–continued...

QUESTION E

Is the health insurance industry regulated by the State or Federal government? Or by both? Am I getting the components that I'm entitled to by law in my health insurance policy? Where can I find out?

Answer

You should read your insurance policy handbook and locate **www.healthcare.gov** for a list of **state healthcare marketplace** websites. See "screen clipping" below:

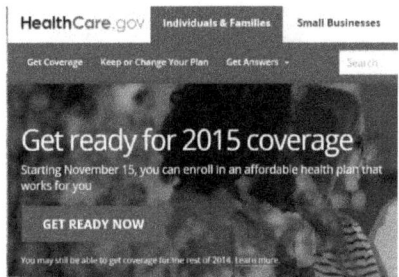

Check your state's **health care market website** for the components of the policy you bought. If you find out there is a discrepancy contact your state's **marketplace consumer help** specialists for help to resolve your issue.

NOTES:

If you have a MEDICARE policy that doesn't have the components you contracted for find the website **www.medicare.gov** The website you seek will say "**official website**." See "screen clipping" next page:

ARE YOU EMPOWERED??? Cynthia Lynn

Query the "**help line**" about your issue.
NOTE:
The website **www.medicare.gov/claims-and-appeals** (as above) is identified as the **Official Medicare.gov** website for **CLAIMS & APPEALS**. See "screen clipping" below:

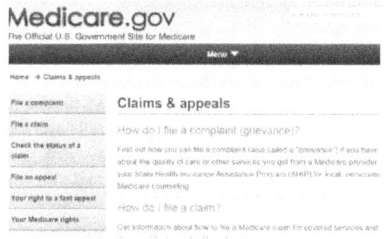

Also the **ATTORNEY GENERAL** of your state may have more information about ways to resolve your issue. **www.attys.org/us-attorney-generals** offers links.

ARE YOU EMPOWERED???   **Cynthia Lynn**

TOPIC: 5. health insurance/other insurance–continued...

QUESTION F

I can't afford to pay the price of the health care policies that are listed in the State and Federal websites. Where can I find out if I am eligible for a health care subsidy?

Answer

Locate **www.healthcare.gov** Call the **"help line"** to find out. See "screen clipping below":

If it's necessary to contact your State **"healthcare marketplace"** you will be given a contact number to call for **INFORMATION ABOUT MEDICAID**.

NOTES:

www.medicare.gov/forms-help-and-resources is a website on the search list that says **Forms, Help & Resources Medicare.gov**. See "screen clipping" below:

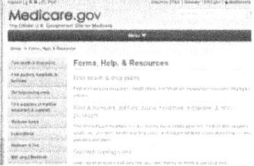

Look on the far left for the 3rd link down to get the information you need.

ARE YOU EMPOWERED???   Cynthia Lynn

TOPIC: 5. health insurance/other insurance–continued...

QUESTION G

I am a senior and would like Part D Drug Insurance, but I can't afford it and have too much in income to fit into the subsidy guidelines. In my area there is a **regional PPO MedicareComplete Choice HMO plan** that offers drug coverage with no premium.

Can I register without worrying about Part D Drug Coverage penalty liability?

Answer

www.medicare.gov/sign-up-change-plans/get-drug-coverage is a Federal government website. See "screen clipping" below:

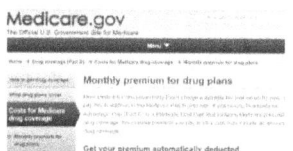

At the bottom of the website it says **"Find someone to talk to."** Chose your state and call the phone number to tell them that you don't want to be liable for a Part D penalty if you chose to register in a **MedicareChoice PPO Part C plan THAT HAS NO PREMIUM**. Don't forget to mention you never had Part D.

NOTE:

Also look in the **Medicare handbook** under **"Drug Plan"**. If you are told that you are not liable for a **Part D ongoing penalty** it's a good idea to ask for written confirmation. Because some of the Health Care Companies offering these plans read you a statement from the Federal Government about liability to the IRS and you have to indicate how you will pay before you are accepted into the program.

ARE YOU EMPOWERED??? Cynthia Lynn

TOPIC: 6. banking-credit/ debit cards

NOTE: see topic 10 about clothes/non clothing items for more about the use of credit cards/debit cards for purchases.

QUESTION A
Are all banks part of the FDIC program and is there a charge for me to participate?
Answer
No to both parts of your question. Locate the website **www.fdic.gov** See "screen clipping" below:

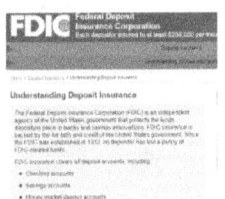

The **FDIC** website has all the information you need. Find the topic you want. For instance, there is **"Bank data"** at the mid-right of the website to find out if your bank is a member.

NOTES:
The website **www.fdic.gov** not only allows you to check your bank to see if it is enrolled in the program you can discover if other money instruments may also be covered. Locate each one to determine how much is covered by **FDIC insurance**. You can also call the **FDIC "call center."** At the bottom left is **"contact"** and you are in another **FDIC website**. See "screen clipping" next page:

ARE YOU EMPOWERED??? Cynthia Lynn

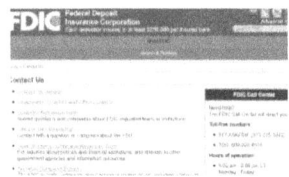

Call to ask your question.

www.wikipedia.org/wiki/Banking_in_the_United_States offers more information about the different banks that are part of the USA banking system some of which are not in the **FDIC bank program**.

If you are relocated to another part of the country and are looking for a local bank try **www.economywatch.com/banks** an "ad sponsored" website that offers more information when your assets are deposited in a bank as to choices other than **FDIC Insurance**.

ARE YOU EMPOWERED???   Cynthia Lynn

TOPIC: 6. banking-credit/ debit cards-continued...

QUESTION B
I have a problem with getting an answer from my bank about CD offerings and APY interest, what does it refer to? And does the Federal government regulate such offerings?

Answer
In answer to the first part of your question the website **www.ehow.com/facts_5776611** gives you some expert information. See "screen clipping" below:

For the answer to the second part of your question about regulation find the website **www.sec.gov/investor/pubs/certific** See "screen clipping" below:

This is a Federal government website that offers information to cover all aspects of your question.

NOTE:
Another Federal government website **www.helpwithmybank.gov/get-answers/bank-accounts/cds-and-cert** also

addresses your issue. See "screen clipping" below:

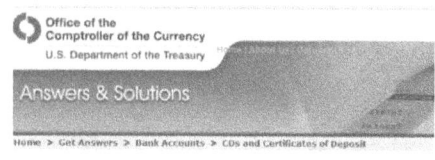

At the bottom right of this website you'll see the phone # for **"The Consumer Assistance Group"** if you have any more questions to ask.

ARE YOU EMPOWERED??? Cynthia Lynn

TOPIC: 6. banking-credit/ debit cards-continued...

QUESTION C

My credit card company told me that if I give my credit card number online I am responsible to call the retailer and ask for a refund. If I cannot get a refund then I have to pay the amount listed for the purchase on my credit card statement.

Is this the policy of all credit card companies or just mine?

Answer

www.creditcards.com/credit-card-news/dispute-credit-card is an ad sponsored website that offers an excellent explanation of the issue you are inquiring about. See "screen clipping" below:

<u>NOTE</u>:

Also contact the Federal government website **www.consumerfinance.gov** to ask **"CONSUMER HELP"** whether your credit card company policies are the same as other credit card companies. See "screen clipping" next page:

ARE YOU EMPOWERED??? Cynthia Lynn

Another Federal government website to contact is **www.helpwithmybank.gov/get-answers/credit-cards** See "screen clipping" below:

For more information you can find the **consumer assistance help line** at the far right bottom of the website.

ARE YOU EMPOWERED???   Cynthia Lynn

TOPIC: 6. banking-credit/ debit cards-continued...

QUESTION D
Is there a Federal government authority who oversees debit card rules and regulations?

Answer
www.usa.gov/topics/money/banking/atm-debit offers comprehensive information to answer your question. See "screen clipping" below:

NOTES:
Politics has been used to mistakenly create the impression President Obama has helped insure more protections for American debit card users, but the President's new policy initiative is "solely" for **Federally issued debit cards**— read the following from the **www.denverpost.com/politics/ci_267501 84/obama-announces**. See "screen clipping" below:

Keep in mind that **credit cards** users in the USA have many more protections, and **debit card** users are still awaiting something equivalent. In Europe the **"Chip system"** referred to in the above article protects either debit cards or credit cards. In the USA only some bank issued **Master Card credit cards** have **"Chip system"** protection.

ARE YOU EMPOWERED???   Cynthia Lynn

TOPIC: 7. cell phone or landline

QUESTION A

My monthly cell phone bill has charges on it that I didn't authorize. I called customer service and they told me that I have to pay the bill or my service will be cut. Who can I call to help me get the charges removed?

Answer

www.ehow.com/facts_6154016_regulates-cell-phone-companies is an "ad sponsored" website that acquaints you with the basics about any regulations governing the **"Wireless Communication Industry"**. See "screen clipping" below:

Scroll down to the **"Other People Are Reading"** for "expert written" informative "ad sponsored" websites that will tell you how to proceed with a complaint to address your issue +   **www.ehow.com/how_5743758_file-complaint-cell-phone-company** is another "ad sponsored" website—see "screen clipping" below:

<u>**NOTES**</u>:

For more information about your issue there are other websites such as **www.naruc.org/Commissions** See "screen clipping" next page:

ARE YOU EMPOWERED??? Cynthia Lynn

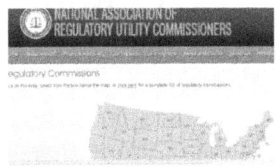

Find the Federal website **www.fcc.gov/complaints** See "screen clipping" below:

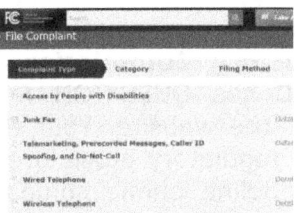

This website will further inform you about what can be done to resolve your issue.

AND
MOST IMPORTANTLY YOU ARE EMPOWERED when you contact the **FCC** to register your complaints about cell phone companies that use billing overcharges as a source of profit.

+ more

Spur your Congressional representatives to regulate cell phone companies with the same consumer protections as landline service providers.

TOPIC: 7. cell phone or landline-continued...

QUESTION B

Is the telecommunications industry regulated? If there are no regulations does that mean they charge any rate they want? Where can I inquire about special rates to ask if I qualify due to income?

Answer

The companies in your area who offer landlines are regulated by your state's **PSC**. For the link **www.naruc.org/Commissions** to your state's **PSC** see QUESTION A for a "screen clipping" of the website. Your **PSC** will inform about their regulatory procedure for raising the rates for landline phone companies. It is the same in each state and the process includes a period of time for "public comment" + "announced in advance" open to the public meetings scheduled around the state.

NOTE:

For the "Lifeline" special rate information and income guideline qualifications, you need to locate **www.fcc.gov/contact-us** See "screen clipping" below:

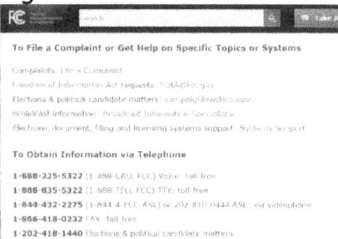

The above "screen clipping" is what you see when you scroll down. If you income qualify you should notify your local landline carrier to apply for "Lifeline."

ARE YOU EMPOWERED???   Cynthia Lynn

TOPIC: 7. cell phone or landline-continued...

QUESTION C
What government authority gives the telecommunications companies permission to serve my community?

And can I ask them to solicit more than 1 company to provide competition?

Answer
www.wikipedia.org/wiki/Competitive_local_exchange_carrier is a recognized public access website offering an excellent overview about the first part of your question. See "screen clipping" below:

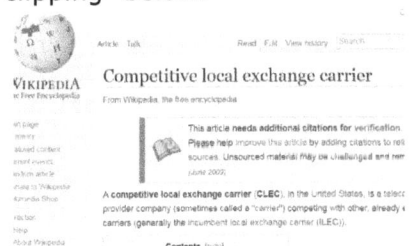

NOTE:
For the ANSWER to the second part of your QUESTION you'll need to ask the **FCC**. Find **www.fcc.gov/contact-us** See "screen clipping" in QUESTION B.

ARE YOU EMPOWERED??? Cynthia Lynn

TOPIC: 7. cell phone or landline-continued...

QUESTION D
What can I do to influence my state and local government to demand competition that will lower rates?

Why aren't there alternatives to what we have now? Like there is with picking a search engine other than Internet Explorer. Why isn't there a uniform global system that will open up the US TELECOMMUNICATIONS market to global competition?

Answer
For the ANSWER to the first part of your question see **www.naruc.org/Commissions** Find the "screen clipping" in QUESTION A/pg. 97), then find the link to your state's PSC to inquire from the help line listed.

And in ANSWER to the second part of your question link to **www.fcc.gov/contact-us** (see "screen clipping" of FCC WEBSITE in QUESTION B/pg.98) and inquire from their help line. Scroll down on their website until you see the contact numbers to call.

ARE YOU EMPOWERED???   Cynthia Lynn

TOPIC: 8. TV/cable or satellite

QUESTION A
Is there any government regulation of the TV broadcast stations? And is there any part of my Local/State or Federal government that regulates the cable or satellite providers?

My community has little competition and our monthly rates are in a bundle. When I inquired about just one service and not the bundle that includes telephone and internet, I was given a rate almost equal to the trio of services.

Who can I complain to about getting just CABLE TV at a rate I can afford instead of a BUNDLE with three other services?

Answer
www.fcc.gov/contact-us can help you with information about regulation of the cable and satellite providers. See website "screen clipping" below:

Scroll down on the screen of this website to find the "contact" phone numbers as shown above.

NOTES:
Also contact your MAYOR or your town's "Board of City Commissioners" Clerk to inquire. Use **www.naruc.org/Commissions** to

ARE YOU EMPOWERED???   Cynthia Lynn

contact your state's Public Service Commission (**PSC**). See "screen clipping" below:

Inquire if your State has any plans to require cable and satellite TV providers to offer a low income basic rate for cable or satellite service.

and

Be **EMPOWERED** to ask your "**network**" **about circulating a PETITION in your area's neighborhood** to require the local City/Town to solicit other cable/satellite providers for more competition in your community. Many communities offer competing providers a tax benefit to provide the community with low income rates for cable/satellite TV service.

ARE YOU EMPOWERED???   Cynthia Lynn

TOPIC: 8. TV/cable or satellite-continued...

QUESTION B

How can I find out more about the DTV alternatives offered by every broadcast station? What if I can't access the broadcast TV stations using the airwaves, can I still get access to the DTV signal as part of my basic cable station lineup? Is there a Local/State or Federal agency with a consumer line to call about my access problem?

Answer

www.fcc.gov/contact-us offers the best source of information about your issue (see QUESTION A for "screen clipping"). Re your QUESTION about access to DTV signals for expert information about DTV television tuners find the "ad sponsored" website **www.ehow.com/about_5372846_kind-tvs-digital-tuners**. See "screen clipping" below:

WARNING: Before you buy your new TV make certain the set you purchase is a **LCD** with **built in DTV tuner** and you won't need a cable box to receive DTV signals via your CABLE or Satellite provider. Prices for 19" LCD TVs are as little as $97. Otherwise your cable or satellite provider will charge you for the HD box on a monthly basis. **Program your TV to AUTO channel and you will see the progress re the number of DTV channels as well as ANALOGUE channels.** To access all the DTV and Analogue channels use the channels + and – on your REMOTE.

ARE YOU EMPOWERED??? Cynthia Lynn

TOPIC: 8. TV/cable or satellite-continued...

QUESTION C
How can I protect myself from being automatically signed up for additional TV services that I didn't order?

I complained to my TV cable provider and the customer service person said it was part of my bundle.

Who can I complain to about what seems to be a hidden component of the bundle I have because this wasn't mentioned in the advertising or by the agent who signed me up.

Answer
The website **www.naruc.org/Commissions** offers links to your state's Public Service Commission (**PSC**) See QUESTION A for "screen clipping." Call the "Consumer" HELP line about your problem and the **PSC** will facilitate resolution with your service provider.

ARE YOU EMPOWERED???   Cynthia Lynn

TOPIC: 8. TV/cable or satellite-continued...

QUESTION D

I live in an apartment building and I am not allowed to get Dish service. I have to use the cable TV provider who wired the building and that cuts off any competition. Can the management of the building do this? What recourse do I have, and where can I find out about my alternatives?

Answer

www.myrateplan.com/sat/condos the "ad sponsored" website offers some information about this issue that may apply to your situation. See "screen clipping" below:

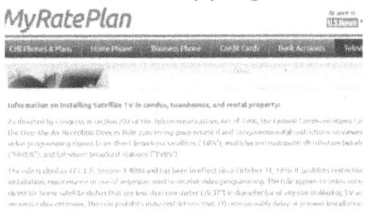

It is noted in the above website that you can place a satellite device on the building but it is limited by size. if you have a patio in a rental property the rule and section given in this website will help when you contact the FCC at **www.fcc.gov/contact-us**. See "screen clipping" below:

Scroll down on the website for the "contact us" phone numbers. Ask the trained consumer specialists for information about regulation of a SATELLITE DISH for your rental apartment. Inquire specifically about your building management's policy.

TOPIC: 9. Internet

QUESTION A

I can't afford the Internet access charge, but I have children who need access because the Internet gives them information they need to excel in school. Who can I call to find out if I am eligible for a government program that helps wage earners like me?

Answer

At **www.naruc.org/Commissions** find your state link. See "screen clipping" below:

Call the CONTACT phone number to ask if your state **PSC** offers a BASIC INTERNET for low income residents.

NOTES:

Another alternative to your situation is to contact your local City/Town Board of Commissioners. Find their website for the direct phone line to the Mayor or to the Town Manager through the City Hall Clerk. And ask when the "open to the public" meeting for the **INTERNET PROVIDER** franchise contract is due for renewal.

and

You are **EMPOWERED** if you and you and your **network** draft a **PETITION** to your City/Town about building a **Wifi Internet** free access for your community. Attend an "open to the public" Town/City meeting to bring this up and present your petition. Keep in mind that your community can offer the INTERNET provider a tax benefit to provide the community with a low income and Senior rate.

ARE YOU EMPOWERED??? Cynthia Lynn

TOPIC: 9. Internet—
continued...

QUESTION B

I'd like to know if only commercial entities can provide Internet access. Does the Federal government have a Department that offers a consumer help line for citizens like me? I'd like to find out who regulates the Internet and if Internet providers charge any rate they want. Also if my local government can provide access with a **community Wifi network** that I can access from my neighborhood?

Answer
www.fcc.gov/contact-us is the regulator for a variety of telecommunications that take place in the USA. See "screen clipping" below:

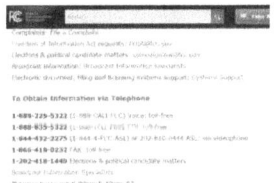

After you scroll down on the screen you will find the "telephone information lines" to ask the **FCC** about your question.
   NOTE:
   See QUESTION A <u>NOTES</u> (2nd paragraph) for suggestions as to how you can be more **EMPOWERED to take action**.

TOPIC: 9. Internet—
continued...
QUESTION C
My Internet provider used to offer "Internet mbps" information whenever I accessed the Internet icon on my desktop lower screen. Now I'm informed that access is either excellent/good/fair. I believe my download speeds are slower than I'd like. When I call my Internet provider the customer service tells me that I can sign up for a faster speed, but when I ask if my download speed is the same for every download I don't get a straight answer.

Are there any regulations about basic internet speeds. Where can I find out about the Internet speed I have?
Answer
www.naruc.org/Commissions offers links to your **PSC** (see QUESTION A for "screen clipping" of that website). Call your **PSC** tollfree number and ask the Customer Service specialist why you can't get that information from your Internet provider.
   NOTE:
   www.fcc.gov/contact-us ("screen clipping" is shown in QUESTION B) has **FCC** "Information Specialists" to ask about each of the "INTERNET mbps" speed offered by your INTERNET provider. Also ask whether there are any government regulations for the "Internet mbps" speeds sold by Internet providers.

ARE YOU EMPOWERED???   Cynthia Lynn

TOPIC: 9. Internet—
continued...

QUESTION D

I pay for monthly Internet service but that doesn't include the fees. I called my Internet provider and I can't get an explanation for the taxes and fees that add about $4 per month to my Internet charge. Where can I find out the reason for those fees and taxes attached to my Internet access?

Answer

www.naruc.org/Commissions offers a link to your state's **PSC** (Public Service Commission) where you will get the answer to your question. See "screen clipping" below:

<u>NOTES</u>:

www.fcc.gov/contact-us (see "screen clipping" in ANSWER B) has "Information Specialists" who can offer more insights about the many fees Internet providers add to increase the cost of your Internet service.

and

You are **EMPOWERED** if you tell the **FCC** that you would like more regulation of the fees which aren't tax based charges the Internet provider can write off as "business related." Also ask if the FCC queries Internet providers about claiming "business expenses" for the same charges that customers pay in addition to the Internet service charge.

ARE YOU EMPOWERED???   Cynthia Lynn

TOPIC: 10 clothing/ other purchases

QUESTION A

I checked on the return policy before I bought the merchandise online and the return policy conditions specified that I notify them why I was returning the product. As required I called customer service to let them know my intentions but when I mentioned that I had thrown away the box and was planning to use my own box securely packaged for the return, I was told they wouldn't accept the return unless I had their box.

My problem is 2-fold: the money was already taken out of my debit card account, and my bank doesn't offer debit credits for purchases I authorized. Who can help me resolve the purchase of a product I can't use? Is there a Local/State or Federal consumer help line to advise me as to what I should do.

Answer

www.dfi.wa.gov/consumers/education/debit is a Washington state website that offers answers about debit card use. See "screen clipping" below:

This website suggests that debit card purchases do need a credit from the retailer to receive credit from your bank issuer, though under

ARE YOU EMPOWERED???   Cynthia Lynn

certain circumstances you may have a way to pursue your claim. As well it is noted that only credit cards have Federally legislated consumer protections.

NOTES:

www.consumerfinance.gov is the Federal government financial regulator of all US financial institutions. Call their **"Consumer Assistance"** help line to ask how to submit a complaint against your bank's debit card policy. See "screen clipping" below:

For more advice as to pursuing your debit card claim with your bank use your "Internet search engine" to locate your state's Department of Financial Services (they also oversee State banks). Call their **"Consumer help"** line and ask for advice as to how you can proceed with your bank to resolve your debit card claim.

Since you purchased online your State's **AG** may oversee Internet purchases, **www.attys.org/us-attorney-generals** offers links to each State. See "screen clipping below:

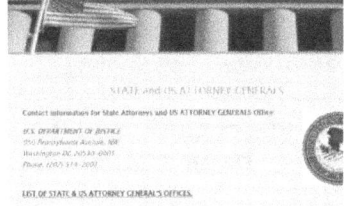

TOPIC: 10 clothing/ other purchases—continued...

QUESTION B
What do I do if I ordered a product online and it was never sent to me yet I was charged for it by my credit card company? I called my credit card company and they told me to get a credit from the online company that sold it to me. Then I called the company that was supposed to send it to me, and they said that they had to research my claim.

A few weeks have since passed but the retail company has not resolved my issue. Is there some way to get my money back?

Answer
You'll need call the merchant again for the purpose of providing evidence of your "good faith" attempt to get a merchant credit and do this:

1. MAKE A LOG OF THE CALL WITH DATE & TIME of your conversation with the merchant customer service/log **first name and last name initial of agent + location of the call center**.

2. If you are still stonewalled **ASK FOR THE CSR SUPERVISOR** and log the call with the same recommended information as stated above.

3. CALL your bank and **Log the call with your bank's customer service agent** (use same method noted above). Tell them about your "good faith" contact with merchant and ask your bank to put

ARE YOU EMPOWERED???   Cynthia Lynn

the purchase in "**dispute**" so you will not have to pay the charge until the investigation by your bank is concluded.

NOTES:

There is a certain number of days for your bank to conclude the investigation of any charge put into "**dispute.**" For information about this + other credit card consumer protections search for the Federal government website **helpwithmybank.gov/index** See "screen clipping" below:

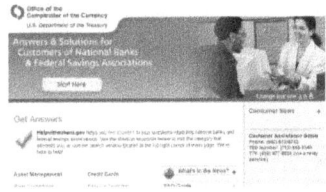

Also see ANSWER A "NOTES" for another suggestion about resolution of your issue with this merchant who refused to issue you a credit for the item never sent to you. You can search for **www.attys.org/us-attorney-generals** (the Federal Attorney General's website) to link to your State's **AG.** Use the tollfree "Consumer complaint" phone line and summarize the issue as follows:

1. I used my credit card for a purchase I never received.

2. I made a good faith effort to get a credit from the merchant which has refused to issue one.

3. Ask for assistance to resolve your issue.

TOPIC: 10 clothing/ other purchases—continued...

QUESTION C

Are Internet purchases regulated by a government agency, or is it a wild west out there for consumers who have problems with the product purchased online?

Answer

When you charge Internet purchases to a **CREDIT CARD** this gives you the best avenue to resolve your issue (see ANSWERS to A and B). Use those website links for more information regarding a resolution to your INTERNET purchase problem.

ARE YOU EMPOWERED???　　　　Cynthia Lynn

TOPIC: 10 clothing/ other purchases—continued...

QUESTION D

I live in an area where there aren't any department stores, and I'm almost half a day away from a major city where there are stores that carry needed items.

It seems that I have to order on the Internet for almost everything including clothing. And then I have a problem with the size if it's made in another country half way around the world. I'm always ordering a size bigger but then nothing I buy fits.

Returning the items are difficult, what can I do? Is there a better way? Where do I find out?

Answer

Unfortunately your problem exists in most of the major Western countries and elsewhere. In the USA consumer laws protect consumers and the Federal Government as well as state governments can HELP to resolve Internet purchase problems. See ANSWERS A and B for the website links that will help and read the A and B ANSWER NOTES.

ARE YOU EMPOWERED???   Cynthia Lynn

TOPIC: 11 Charity donations

QUESTION A

How can I be sure that my money is going to the cause I am donating to? Is there a government agency that regulates Charity groups? How can I get in touch with them to determine if the group is legitimate?

Answer

The website that best answers your question is **www.charitynavigator.org/index.cfm** See "screen shot" below:

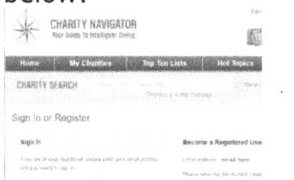

Put in the name of the charity in the search screen or use one of the links on the top ribbon to find more information. When you link to the "Home" page you can find charities by category. Scroll down to the bottom of the screen to contact that organization if you want more information.

NOTE:

If you suspect that a CHARITY group is NOT LEGITIMATE query for ADVICE from the "consumer complaint" line of your state Attorney General. Use the website **www.attys.org/us-attorney-generals** to link to your State's AG. See "screen clipping" below:

If you have proof contact the above website and tell the CSR all you know.

ARE YOU EMPOWERED??? Cynthia Lynn

TOPIC: 11 Charity donations-
continued...

QUESTION B

I heard that it is possible to get a tax refund for my donation. Can I qualify for a deduction on my State and Federal tax forms?

Answer

www.irs.gov/uac/Contact-Your-Local-IRS-Office. is the website to locate to answer your question. See "screen clipping" below:

Use the link "Help & Resources" on the far right of the grey information ribbon. SCROLL down to find the LINK to your state IRS location. And find the tollfree phone number to ask the information expert for the Federal TAX CREDIT form # to print out online to include with both Federal and State tax forms. Keep in mind that you have to Itemize to ask for that credit.

NOTE:

www.irs.gov/Businesses/Small-Businesses-&-Self-Employed/State-Links-1 offers a list of State tax offices. See "screen clipping" below:

TOPIC: 11 Charity donations-
continued...

QUESTION C

Will the charity I donate to give me a receipt that will be accepted by the State and Federal tax authorities? Or do I have to specifically request a receipt when I donate?

Answer

www.ehow.com/how_2049261_get-charity-receipt is an "ad sponsored" website that offers expert advice about your question. See "screen shot" below:

NOTE:

www.ehow.com/list_7349199 offers a list of "qualified IRS CHARITIES." See "screen clipping" below:

ARE YOU EMPOWERED??? Cynthia Lynn

TOPIC: 12 religious tithe

QUESTION A

My income is so low that I am having trouble making my weekly tithe and sometimes I have to take the money for a donation out of my weekly food purchases.

I think that others in my social network have the same problem but no one talks about it openly. Where can I go for advice as to what I should do?

Answer

The answer to your **QUESTION** is in the realm of **OPINION** and not fact, but www.freemoneyfinance.com/2007/02/how_to_tithe the "ad sponsored" website gives one opinion. See "screen clipping" below:

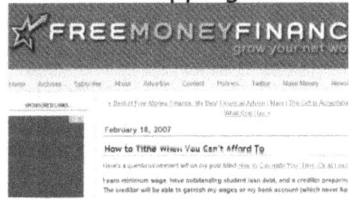

www.tithing.com/blog/top-10-reasons-why-tithing-is-not-required offers another OPINION. See "screen clipping" below:

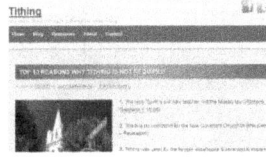

TOPIC: 12 religious tithe-
continued...

QUESTION B

Who at my place of worship is in charge of levying the amount of my weekly tithe? Can I get some information as to what other ways I can give something rather than money?

Answer

www.wikipedia.org/wiki/Tithe gives an excellent overview about this topic. See "screen clipping" below:

Use your search engine's "search slot" to locate the "ad sponsored" expert advice website **www.ehow.com/about_4679788_what-definition-tithing** Scroll down to the bottom where there are 3 links for **ehow** websites on the same topic with more answers to your question:

1.www.ehow.com/about_4679788_what-definition-tithing
2.www.ehow.com/facts_6087949_tithing
3.www.ehow.com/about_4596486_is-tithing-biblical See the "screen clippings" on the following page:

ARE YOU EMPOWERED???   **Cynthia Lynn**

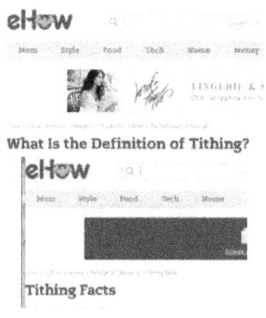

What Is the Definition of Tithing?

Tithing Facts

s Tithing Biblical?

ARE YOU EMPOWERED??? Cynthia Lynn

TOPIC: 12 religious tithe-
continued...

QUESTION C

Is a weekly or yearly tithe a charity donation? Can I use the amount I give as a tax deduction? Is my place of worship required to show how much I donate if the State and Federal tax authorities want proof of my donation?

Answer

For the **ANSWER** to the first part of your **QUESTION** see "ANSWER B," for the second, **www.uslaw.com/library/Estate_Planning/ Tithing_Gifts_Church_Valid_Receipt**, see "screen clipping" below:

www.irs.gov/Businesses/Small-Businesses-&-Self-Employed/State-Links-1 has a list of State tax Offices—see the "screen clipping" at "ANSWER B," and use the CONTACT phone number at the website of your State tax office to ask about their tax policies for claiming a religious tithe.

SECTION THREE

HOW DID YOU BECOME EMPOWERED???

Inspired To Action

CONSUMER Action TOPICS

selected "thinkingoutloudan" blogs

the challenge to keep empowered

HOW DID YOU BECOME EMPOWERED???

You were skeptical that consumers anywhere can get what they pay for in this 21st century era of big businesses that spend thousands of dollars to prevent "Government" from legislating more consumer protection laws. You found it was to difficult to pursue your right to receive what you paid for.

You wondered how refusing to accept anything less than what you are promised will bring change in your life. Nevertheless you tried this "step by step" and started with no longer accepting the right of big businesses to cheat you out of what you paid for.

And something happened.

You became EMPOWERED by success, and you used the most important tool I gave you: the **Network—they** shared the burden of researching sources of advice, and these new sources initiated new opportunities. All at once you discovered that by better managing your income you could find the way to a better quality of life.

NOW you are ready to make the other necessary changes in your life that once seemed impossible.

LET'S SUM UP

EMPOWERMENT

1. You have a new top priority: now **you** make time to use the **Internet** to enrich **your** knowledge about what's happening that may affect **your** life. **You** are no longer living **your** life for the "short term." **You** are intent on the "long term" and are making the changes that once seemed impossible.

2. You aren't discouraged by setbacks because you know that a setback is a **challenge** to brainstorm with **your Network** + the initiative for how-to find new ways to get the answers **you** need with your Internet "search engine." **YOU** use the power of words to "ask the question" that **you** know will lead to more answers. Because you are **EMPOWERED TO FIND SOLUTIONS that once seemed too high a hurdle to surmount.**

3. You have a greater sense of satisfaction every day. No longer are **you** besieged by that sense of emptiness and dissatisfaction with what **you** have achieved. **You** are more sure of **yourself** and **your** ability to get through life. **You** know no matter what happens **you** can control the outcome with "**step by step self-action.**"

Inspired to ACTION

You are now inspired to contact and prod **your** "Government" to give everyone a chance to expand horizons + make the changes that will improve the quality of life.

You are now **EMPOWERED** and **inspired** to make a future of better possibilities by getting involved as a concerned citizen who joins with others to draft petitions to elected "Government" representatives. Now **you** communicate with **your** elected representatives regularly to inform and educate them to accomplish changes in the laws to further improve everyone's quality of life.

You now take time to read and search the Internet for news that will negatively impact **your** quality of life + **you** are keeping abreast of company mergers that are intended to alter and change regulations to allow service providers to raise rates and engage in unfair consumer practices. You are now **inspired** to make time to send your comments to the "Government" regulators who are charged with a mandate to oversee the businesses that are providing essential services to your community.

ARE YOU EMPOWERED???   Cynthia Lynn

You are now aware that what happens in **your** community affects you too and that all citizens have an **obligation** to advocate for legislation that can create a better future for everyone.

You now know that if **you** live in a nation with laws to benefit both rich and poor everyone is more prosperous which creates unexpected opportunities to pursue what **you** never thought was possible.

ARE YOU EMPOWERED???   **Cynthia Lynn**

Topics that NEED consumer Action

My view of the world

The reason I started my BLOG was out of frustration with the "Pundits" and unelected "Journalists" who remain consistently EMPOWERED by their privileged position in society as the defender of everyone's rights. Yet they don't respect my right to have a contrary opinion and it bothers me that they want me to live in their world + they want me to see their world as the best world.

I am including some of my selected BLOGS with consumer topics that need action. My Blog was written off the cuff and I didn't do much to edit out the imperfections. Though for inclusion in this book I have edited out the most glaring wrong word choices as well as grammatical errors. I've also cut some blogs and added continuing portions.

It's my hope that what I have written provokes you to think for yourself. If you have an opinion contrary to mine let me know, but keep in mind we live in a democracy, and we must find a way to live with others who don't agree with our view of the world. I also believe

ARE YOU EMPOWERED??? Cynthia Lynn

everyone has to start "thinkingoutloudan" + get involved as a lawful activist to change laws and regulations to improve the quality of life. I know we can use our democratic system to contact elected officials to tell them what we think. One of the benefits of living in a democratic society is to voice opinions contrary to those elected officials who aren't listening to you and the citizen network of the like minded. Don't forget when you are **EMPOWERED** you make a regular practice of checking facts on the Internet with the "how-to" tools available in this book. Read all you can about what is happening in your "Government" because laws passed have unintended consequences, but each of us has a voice that can affect a change. Keep in mind that in a democratic nation prosperity is based on compromise to achieve benefits for all, and no one group of individuals has the right to dictate their way above all.

ARE YOU EMPOWERED???   Cynthia Lynn

Selected edited "thinkingoutloudan" blogs 2013

There are lots of talking heads on the Sunday a.m. talking heads shows. Like for instance, MEET THE PRESS. But I see them all the time wherever there are the so called "members of the press" and they want to be my conscience. I'm sick and tired of having these anointed and unelected by anyone but their Newspapers/TV Broadcast brand employers who want their "press" to tell me what to think about and how to redirect my conscience.

My problem is that they aren't listening to me or to you. I'm like everyone else. I'm a "common person" who is tired of the rhetoric that surrounds me on the airwaves. It's a growing tower of Babel.

We have the politicians who speak with "forked tongues." And they have their campaigns financed by the ones who are "shadow governments" financing the "lobbies." Sadly, at the time of the inception of the US Constitution the makers of the "Constitution" of this US of A were thinking in very small numbers of the population. Certainly, they didn't plan for the population "economics" of the "K Street Lobby Groups" usually composed of former members of Congress making "hay" while this 21st century sun shines. Our "founders" idea of groups of people banding together to speak to government about their concerns was not created with the large dollar signs that draw former government employees who gather their close Congressional contacts into the trawl of "K Street Lobby groups" to receive campaign money and untraceable "favors."

Those groups who populate Washington's "K Street" are now high salaried employees

ARE YOU EMPOWERED???   Cynthia Lynn

who have had a political connection and their commercial connections are legion. For instance, newspapers have a "freedom of the Press" lobby but they also hire the "talking head" members of the "press" who speak out to redirect my conscience.
To be continued...
2013

I'm distressed by the chutzpah of the "press" especially when it puts forth an ideal democracy that often has nothing to do with those parts of the world composed of tribal societies who exist in tandem with the supreme interpreters of their religious tenets. And even more so when the USA "powerful press" tout going to war for the principles of "democracy" that 3rd world countries composed of tribal societies aren't familiar with. To me it's clear that whatever exists in a tribal society must have the acceptance of the interpreters of their religious tenets, but that can bring on another timely blog on a future day.

Though the other day I was cheered when I watched the "public TV channel" and I saw pundits who were members of that "powerful press" including a former BTO in the political establishment + the magazine owner + the elderly moderator who produces this particular PBS pundit show. Because all of them admitted what I know, and probably what you know too. These "pundits" were talking about how "globalization" was supposed to create "one world in peace and prosperity" + they addressed the fact that the definition of "free trade globalization" was based on the concept of a "world in peace" manufacturing goods rather than war. As if to show how that was supposed create more jobs for US workers, these same "pundits" referenced the failure of Congress to remember that this US of A had

ARE YOU EMPOWERED???   Cynthia Lynn

already experienced the disastrous effect of our first "free trade" agreement which was not a "fair to the US" Nixon's "trade with China agreement" because the closing of US textile mills was the result. The "pundit" former BTO in the political establishment that most of the "powerful press" doesn't agree with pointed out how shipping our jobs to China saved money for the Corporate textile mill owners and it was passed along in price savings to US consumers who were delighted.

In the politics of "free trade globalization" there are winners and losers, for instance, the then Senate majority leader who was against "free trade" with our neighbors was in the last year of his term in office, and for the primaries he received no financial support from his own political party + he couldn't raise any funds from his usual sources.

It was rumored that Corporate "K Lobby" money finished the career of that faithful public servant, though I am left wondering if the now so highly ascended "BTO," whose career and influence flourished after the passage of his "free trade" with our neighbors, knew that factories in the USA would close and those jobs shipped overseas where labor was cheap, rather than bring jobs to the well paid US union workers. I'm suspicious because this "ascended on high" in the political establishment BTO regularly does focus groups touting "free trade globalization" with those who also have ascended very high in the "global Corporate" establishment.

To be continued...
2013

The consequences of "globalization" did effect the political party in control of the Presidency during the final stretch of the "so-called" prosperity term of the now BTO person

ARE YOU EMPOWERED??? Cynthia Lynn

who has ascended so very high up, because the unions were angry that many US workers lost their jobs. In exchange for campaign money "Corporate donors" wanted lots more trade agreements and got what they wanted when they helped elect a new Congress and President from the opposing political party.

The public TV channel's "pundit group" BTO magazine owner cited statistics to show that now the unions have helped elected another political party who claims to be the "party of the middle class," the only jobs our country can count on are in the low wage service sector, but these workers were the majority of workers included in the current "lowest unemployment" figures as presented by the "party of the middle class" now currently in control of the Senate and the Presidency.

The magazine owner + the others included in this PBS "pundit" TV production, except for the 1 who usually disagrees, indicated that the "party of the middle class" grants "access" perks to a powerful "shadow" government of "nerds" from "Silicon Valley," but for some reason these same "shadow" government of "nerds" from "Silicon Valley" aren't pressured to undertake retraining US workers, nor to be involved in US Community College programs training college level students for the technical level of knowledge needed to excel in this "global society." What is expected of this "shadow" government of "nerds" from "Silicon Valley" includes campaign money + aid with their expertise for gathering voting blocks to organize prior to the oncoming elections, but what all of "Silicon Valley" wants is a Senate in support of granting "global world workforce" visas for the import to the USA of all the labor they need which they claim US workers aren't qualified to fulfill and they continue to ignore the "why."

To be continued...

2013

There is a USA "Tiger mom" who wrote a book about her "Tiger mom" methods and mentioned that those once 3rd world societies are now "globalized countries" who are the focus of "Silicon Valley's nerds" to hire them to work in the USA on special visas.

It's no secret that Silicon Valley's "shadow government" is gearing to hire those now happily modernized and industrialized 3rd world "globalized" newly educated at their government expense ready to enter directly into the USA, thanks to a new set of special visas for workers from nations with "tiger moms." Yet this nation's "powerful press" has failed to write about this. And here in this US of A, our moms and dads teach their kids to court "pleasure" + how to collect debt to get all the bling they can. How do they get it? They game the economics of our US of A aimed at "spenders" not "savers." The smart and government savvy moms and dads apply for tax subsidies—some don't have any money because they spend it all to keep their incomes low enough to qualify for subsidized whatever including the now government mandated health care.

This may all sound like a rant, but thanks to the biggest lobby "shadow government" which is on "K Street" in Washington D.C., the Fed keeps interest rates at 0% to stimulate business and this is the policy that continues the inequality of the top 1%, who have large blocks of investments, yet pay little in taxes when compared to the average wage earner. In defense of its policy the Fed claims that the nation's "pension funds" benefit from a "bull"

ARE YOU EMPOWERED???   Cynthia Lynn

market, yet when there's another 2008 disaster, the 1% will know in advance and get out, leaving the nation's "pension funds" to hold the empty bag of worthless stocks to cash in at pennies on the dollar. We can't win if we play fair and square in this US of A since now liars and cheats rule the roost, and thanks to the Fed 0% interest rate Banks lend at 3-4% + corporations use the "K Street" tax loopholes to avoid paying their share of Federal tax.

The political watch of the party that says it is for the "middle class" and the "powerful press" who leans toward it have not bothered to address the reasons why this US of A income inequality persists, perhaps it's time for a change toward truth and fairness.

2013

Have you noticed that the hen house of the consumer has been decimated by the foxes sent in by those in "Government" who claimed to champion consumer protection, though I'm "thinkingoutloudan" particularly about the lack of regulation for the telecommunications industry. Initially the notion of "deregulation" was touted as a "benefit for consumers" and that era began with Airline Deregulation. The **www.wikipedia.org/wiki/Airline_Deregulation_Act** website offers this historical view:

"The Airline Deregulation Act is a United States 1978 Federal law intended to remove government control over fares, routes and market entry (of new airlines) from commercial aviation. The Civil Aeronautics Board's powers of regulation were phased out, eventually allowing passengers to be exposed to market forces in the airline industry. The Act, however, did not remove or diminish the regulatory powers of the Federal Aviation

ARE YOU EMPOWERED??? Cynthia Lynn

Administration (FAA) over all aspects of air safety..."

When airfares went way down, and all at once flying became cheaper than taking the bus, the public was ecstatic. When big airlines were broken up and competition fueled the race to price airfares to the lowest range consumers were hooked on the drug of "deregulation" in any service and provider industry. Over the following years Federal legislators in Congress capitulated to the ever more powerful "K Street" Washington D. C. Lobby groups, with the result that Federal government regulations were opened wide to allow "deregulation" in other service industries like electricity.

It wasn't long until Congress decided government had a mandate to break up the conglomerates, but keep in mind the smart foxes of "K Street" chose the airline industry to deregulate first, so as to quell public fears. Though it seems plausible the airline industry knew something had to be done to add to the number of flying passengers that had lagged in growth for too many years. As well, the sharp "K Street" analysts had no doubt about the success of their ventures. They planned to cite proof of a successful and publically popular "Airline Deregulation Act" to their Congressional cronies, as a way to convince a majority of the service and provider regulators to herald a new era of deregulation prosperity for business and consumer groups alike.

I remember there was a time before "Globalization" took over when the "Government" was more eager to protect citizen consumers, but within closed doors that "K Street" Washington Lobby burrowed deep in discussion with powerful Congressional committee chairs. That's when traffic in the halls and corridors of Congress increased to a

ARE YOU EMPOWERED??? Cynthia Lynn

flurry of "K Street" Lobby groups intent on getting government regulators into the fray of an era of unbridled commerce seeking to convince the "protectors of the consumer" the "regulators," how calling for legislation with a "trap door" can allow for "no regulation" + leave only market forces creating another plethora of consumer benefits.

To be continued...
2013

The "K Street" Lobby Groups were artful foxes raiding the consumer henhouse—they knew what they were doing when the electric monopolies were broken up, here's how it was according to "here's how deregulation works" **www.electric.com/deregulation-of-energy**:

"...Energy deregulation is the reason you can shop for an electricity provider in the first place. It gives you the power to choose your provider, and ultimately, how much you'll end up paying for energy. The deregulation of energy affects over half of the country—some for electricity, some for natural gas, and some for both. These open markets benefit consumers by driving competition. When energy suppliers compete for your money, you win. The more you know about what they're offering and why, the more you could possibly save in the long run."

Everyone who pays high electric bills today knows that what is still being sold as a competition "boon" didn't bring lower rates, but it wasn't immediately apparent that the consumer didn't benefit when these new electric companies were created by the banking foxes like J. P. Morgan and the Goldman Sachs crowd just like eggs created in vitro. Currently in 2013 just in one US State there can be as

ARE YOU EMPOWERED???   Cynthia Lynn

many as 4 or 5 electric companies all charging much higher rates predicated on "special surcharges" allowed by the State electric regulators (the PSC) during fuel shortages and weather fluctuations. And that's when an electric provider claims the need to pay for their original big investment. As everyone knows most US states grant franchises to 1 electric company per square area. Often these companies can also regulate in other parts of a State that isn't contiguous.

The enormous $$ investment stakes for the original big investors included building a facility from scratch, but the original investors knew the profit factor was also enormous. One can presume that the "K Street" lobby commissioned an engineering analysis to come up with a business model of all profit and no loss for an electric company unique perfect business. Which is how all business expense for these electricity providers is paid by customers, and that includes maintenance of any existing wires left behind by the "deregulated State-wide" electric company. And with no improvements necessary. For every USA electric provider it's just fix and maintain sections that wear and tear. Any new wiring is usually underground and is paid for by the city or county that wants it, or by the developers of new home communities.

Since this electric company business model generates a hefty profit for shareholders without improvement of infrastructure, now you know why the electric grid in this US of A is no longer adequate + why in this 21st century of speed in all things, days and weeks are necessary to recover power lost due to storms. You also may not know that those original telephone-like poles with wires that are subject to nature's furies were put up by a "never

ARE YOU EMPOWERED??? Cynthia Lynn

regulated" but then acquired by the newly "deregulated" State-wide electric conglomerates.

To be continued...
2013

The many splendored saga of deregulation continues with the biggest prize: telecommunications giant AT&T which was saved for last, because by then there was a hint of a plethora of new telecommunications technology. It was expected these technology discoveries would herald for each consumer a way to telecommunicate the written word + add another gadget to the consumer tool box. This "gadget" was something featuring a miniature screen that could not only be viewed, but would serve as a unique method of communication, and not by wire, yet between individuals in a "globally" unwired world.

The telecommunications giant AT & T was broken up just like the electric companies were, into state-wide confusions. And just like the electric industry, telephone rates rose considerably + so did the confusion of consumers. In some States now there are as many as 6 different telephone companies. These new communications entities were all hatched by the likes of the J. P. Morgan and Goldman Sachs crowd in their lab of "in vitro" investor offerings, as well, every telephone company now has their own telephone book with a different area code.

Nothing of the magnitude or confusion as with service provider industries occurred with the deregulated legacy airlines, mainly due to new market entries, but it wasn't long before the older legacy airlines were no longer viable, and many US airline employees lost their jobs even their pensions in the legacy airlines rush to bankruptcy. The few legacy airlines that

ARE YOU EMPOWERED???   Cynthia Lynn

managed to recapitalize rose to become market players, though many communities lost their airline service at the same time the bus service industry was deregulated. At the beginning of the 21st century, bus service in some rural area didn't exist, nor did a public airport that wasn't at least 100-200 miles or more out of the way of each community. Eventually many rural communities discovered they had no transportation other than their cars, and since there were no taxis either, due to shrinking rural rider base, in most rural communities a car was a necessity. Worse was coming because gas prices were climbing and the USA as a country where transportation of all sorts was swift and easy was no more.

The new era of the investment industry players who became banks that can't fail were by then in control of the world's financial future + the consumer hen was unawares that their golden boom of prosperity with no government deficits would soon end.

To be continued...
2013

Maybe you've forgotten that hedge funds and such were creations of the Capitalistic economic genius of J. P. Morgan and Goldman Sachs crowd who had hatched all those "in vitro" deregulation creations that changed the nature of the USA provider industries. As well, so stealthy these "too big to fail" investment firms were converted to commercial investment banks by the "super foxes," who penetrated into the top reaches of our government during the early years of the 1990's, when the President with a golden tongue and not yet disgraced used his persuasive powers that could charm birds out of trees. He convinced Congress what the nation needed was a forward looking "Housing Administration"

ARE YOU EMPOWERED??? **Cynthia Lynn**

headed by a Director sitting in the President's Cabinet who was a member of an up and coming minority. The golden tongue with his then Secretary of the Treasury counseled repeal of the 1933 Glass-Steagall Banking Act that rightfully separated commercial banks from securities activity and from any such affiliations, as no longer in the best interest of the nation's continued prosperity with no deficits.

The consumer hen was oblivious to the foxes when the "hedge funds" created by the J. P. Morgan et al crowd rose like snakes to wind around the housing industry with a series of mortgage spinoffs. The foxes gained complete control of the consumer hen house when the Gramm-Leach-Bliley Act repealed the Glass-Steagall Banking Act. By then banks were too heavily invested in mortgage spinoffs + the housing industry was at an all time high, with new homes built faster than people could move into them. It wasn't long before banks were stuck with a glut and the newest minority member of the Cabinet sprung up with an idea to benefit those who never had the opportunity to own a home.

This new "every man and woman consumer plus home ownership" was advocated as a **nation-wide path to equality. And the sale of** homes to minorities, whether they had money to put down or a constant source of income, equaled the playing field between the have's and the have not's. The "K Street" Lobby groups got involved so that Congress blessed this newest national housing initiative with Fanny Mae to supervise the granting of complex financial instruments for sale to banks + Fanny Mae decided to invest in some of the mortgages, as well as oversee the gathering of other government subsidies, to fill in any

ARE YOU EMPOWERED???   Cynthia Lynn

homeowner income gaps so as to guarantee the loans for these now overly complex mortgages instruments called derivatives.

Thus these new mortgage investment vehicles were hatched by hedge funds, who kept figuring out more complex financial instruments, to cover an over abundance of new homes nation wide. Luring those wanting a home to accept the mortgages conceived by the hedge funds that locked in steadily rising rates not explained to the eager prospective homeowners. Surely you remember when investment banking giant Lehman Bros. failed, the panic brought out the foxes in the hen house ready to spur the printing presses of the Federal Reserve to come to the rescue. Only the taxpayers would lose their 401K pensions swimming in the red of bleeding derivative deficits. The bank shareholders were shielded from losses, but each taxpayer was charged with paying for something they didn't know was happening years earlier, back when that golden tongued President of prosperity reigned.

To be continued...
2013

The foregoing series of blogs have chronicled how deregulation benefitted the financial industry and not the consumer + detailed the stealth growth of the J. P. Morgan and Goldman Sachs crowd of giant investment banks "too big to fail." They created all of the newest conglomerates that have replaced more of the nation's service and provider deregulated entities, now merging into newer energy replacement conglomerates funding gas produced by a method known as "fracking," are also involved in worldwide investment opportunities for what is taking place in the US to find other means of supplying the nation + the global world with power sources.

ARE YOU EMPOWERED???   Cynthia Lynn

Another result of the J. P. Morgan crowd is that its offshoots are tentacles so deeply embedded into the nation's major telecommunications prime industries, that the "doing business as" list is embedded into the complexities of global telecommunications corporations now in one voice advocating the cutting of land telephone lines "in favor of the airwaves." In some USA rural communities worn land line wires are being phased out in favor of cell phone controlled transmission of sound via advanced technological wonders to encompass our bodies with wearable sound devices + more "encased in cell phones" and the "yet to be designed" to assume even newer shapes for purchase with higher prices for all— the consumer is left with a choice to make as to how fast to drive themselves into debt to "communicate."

Now the necessity of a telephone "at the ear" or "a device on the ear" is the only way to survive in this world of banks that can't fail + national major stores whose security is lax because the Federal government hasn't made them beef up. Nor has the Federal government mandated the nation's banks to issue credit cards with the European Union's chip system until mid-2015. And US merchants are not obligated to install the special credit card payment terminals until sometime in 2016. Although Federal bank regulators are aware the "debit plastic" option can more easily compromise a consumer's identity, no action has been taken to include it in the "chip" mandate, other than for Federally issued debit plastic.

To be continued...
2013

Apropos to my labored explanation of how US consumers slept while their consumer hen

ARE YOU EMPOWERED???   Cynthia Lynn

house was invaded by the "too big to fail" banking foxes, I was experiencing one of those months when I couldn't afford to buy more cell phone minutes on my "pay as you go" service. Since I was determined not to buy what I couldn't afford, even if I could charge it with plastic, I found out from personal experience how the J. P. Morgan et al crowd of foxes had gobbled me up too.

My lack of communications ordeal was acerbated by what happened during the year 2002 when landline pay phone service was phased out in my community, thus, I was in a terrible fix at 9 p.m. the day before Labor Day 2013 in this "live on credit pay as we can" society. Doggedly I was sticking to my budget for the month regardless, and when I used my almost run out of minutes cell phone to seek out my landline customer service about repair for my unresponsive landline, I was depending on one of those deregulated foxy dual communications giant corporations to bail me out of my budget dilemma. I was very surprised when I wasn't placed on hold, also I was able to explain the nature of my problem, as well, I was connected promptly to the technical service and my landline was tested.

The problem was in the wiring according to the line tester, but I was informed a technician had to determine if the wiring was outside or inside my premises + I was told those technicians had gone home for the day. It seemed like good news when I was given an appointment promptly for the following day, but when I remembered this was the US Labor Day holiday and mentioned it, I was immediately reassured that special contractor technicians on duty for holidays would come to fix my landline phone wiring problem by noon at the latest. Very early on Labor Day morning

ARE YOU EMPOWERED??? Cynthia Lynn

while I was making some coffee I started inquiring regularly with the few remaining minutes of my cell phone "pay as you go" plan, and each time I was assured my appointment was listed in the job schedule, but when the 12 noon repair time failed to materialize, I used up my remaining cell phone minutes to make call center inquiries. One customer service person said, "The problem from a line test appears to be outside your building." A few hours later, one grumpy having to work on our American Labor Day even if they were in another country working as an employee told me, "The problem might be inside your premises and you don't have a line protection plan." At this point I realized I didn't keep the itemized bills but instead I had a log of the amounts I paid and I hung up more worried. An hour later, I tried making another inquiry call, but my "pay as you go" cell phone was silent and I had no way of telling if I would have to be responsible for the wire problem.

The range of my debt to this dual land line/cell phone telecommunications fox created by J. P. Morgan and their ilk was a constant source of worry, though I felt a little more positive when I was able to borrow a cell phone from a neighbor and could call the repair service every few hours. Each time I was told there was no way to get in touch with the dispatch of repair persons + they had no updates about my scheduled appointment, which started out as no later than noon, but had extended into the dinner hour. Although I knew no repair technician was on the way at 8 p.m. I telephoned the call center to see what customer service would tell me. Again I was connected to another foreign call center and this employee told me that no repair technician had picked up my repair ticket + no one had

ARE YOU EMPOWERED??? Cynthia Lynn

checked to see if the problem was in the main cable switch center. He suggested hopefully, "Maybe tomorrow," and I remembered to ask for a direct dial tollfree number to the repair department, which he gave to me without a problem.

The point of my personal story is to present the truth about these powerful telecommunications giants who are increasingly allowed by the FCC to set their own standards for service. Though this all worked out for me, I was at the mercy of one of those "foxy" telecommunications "in vitro" creations of the "too big to fail" Goldman Sachs crowd—and this "foxy" had hired "out of country" employees who did their best to get me to pay for the problem. I was saved by some Local USA honest union workers who made certain that I wasn't outfoxed by a "global" company that wasn't about to give up any source of profit, even a manufactured one. And American consumers are scammed by these very foxy telecommunications giants who can hire foreign employees willing to do what they want. Keep in mind, those are "in vitro" telecommunications global entities who are confident that many "Governments" will NOT regulate them and they have clear bottom line motives. Here in the USA either they are reigned-in by the FCC + legislated by Congress to the status of "public utility," or they will succeed in cutting land line service to all communities in the nation within the next three years.

2013

The USA stopped being the world's "moral policeman" when the world realized the USA had suckered them with worthless mortgages transformed into financial wunderkind instruments sold to banks worldwide. The

ARE YOU EMPOWERED???   Cynthia Lynn

tragedy of the United States fallen from the grace of a "moral policeman" for the world bears examination as the prime example of a nation in "false economic prosperity" that lost its mojo in so many ways. It was happening on my watch but I was too busy to notice this current USA's economic dilemma was a-brewing during the 1990's, but I can be comforted by the fact that what was about to happen was hidden even from the most astute economists.

The USA taxpayers had to bail out AIG Corporation insurer of the world and we took the hit in many other ways too. For instance, while the part of the Western world we had rescued with the Marshall Plan were prepared with an adequate social safety net to survive well enough to celebrate a higher standard of living by the year 2013, in 2008 Americans saw their 401K pensions drowned in a bond and stock market gone south. Now the rest of the world knows that Americans are having trouble getting by on their low wages + there is no longer a viable middle class. The disparities gap between incomes of Americans has widened to what is now perceived as the "top 1%" paying the least taxes, yet seeing the most gains in income thanks to the Federal Reserve policy of a roaring bull stock market.

In 2013, thanks to a Congress that since 2008 has been involved in "legacy legislation" rather than an economic laser focus, neither political party gave a thought to regulating all telecommunications as utilities. That's why Americans are further than ever separated from participation in the high speed "global Internet." All due to a Congress who keeps "hands off" the telecommunications big business corporations and the cable companies. Despite that telecommunications business

ARE YOU EMPOWERED??? Cynthia Lynn

practices are choking the USA into an "isolation box" of slow Internet speeds, and no infrastructure improvements, until the need for technology advances already commonly used in the "global world" allows them to ask for more special considerations to allow for extensive investment—now a unique creation of tiers of service for the business of delivering it is on the telecommunications industry's agenda.

So what are our elected law makers doing???

To be continued...
2013

Although Americans are in an "isolation box" of slow Internet mbps speeds due to telecommunications Corporate greed for more profit and no investment, the political party that holds the Senate has not bothered to legislate any laws to mandate fair pricing and basic mbps speed regulations for the Internet. Nor does any political party seem to care that many Americans aren't connected to the "global world." In eastern states like New York there are areas upstate where there is no Internet service. According to a front page article printed in *The New York Times* Saturday 9/7/2013 edition, there's a party in power push for telecommunications privacy—a N. J. Congressman from the political party that currently controls the Senate and Presidency recently put forth a bill aimed to stop NASA from gaining access to encrypted communications via e-mail. It's something this Congressman believes polls well in his liberally inclined and possibly libertarian district—a + for his reelection in 2014, and just like other politicians, he is not bothered by the US lag in "global" Internet communications, or the lack of consumer fair pricing in an unregulated very "foxy" telecommunications industry. Meanwhile

ARE YOU EMPOWERED??? Cynthia Lynn

Google is happily reading the e-mails of their subscribers to place ads that add to Google's bottom line. It also seems that the White House is partial to the "shadow government" of Silicon Valley who benefit from the deeds of the "K Street" crowd. Let's include Yahoo, Facebook and all the others who bask in the solace of bottom line fortunes. All the while Americans have to worry about the basics of food, shelter + educating the young who are increasingly alienated from the adult establishment. The nation's youth must know the Europeans are working and can rest easy from cradle to grave to enjoy societal perks such as month long annual vacations, perhaps they see no hope for the future and that's why they prefer to get high on the latest street drug. Keep in mind that European citizens gladly pay taxes to have income security, and they have empowered their legislators to regulate the big corporations who do business in their country and mandate big business to pay their fair tax share.

Only in the United States are there "K Street" lobbies that actively promote Congressional cooperation for Corporate "tax loopholes" which allow the richest and the biggest of USA corporations to stash their money in companies formed overseas, just for that purpose. For example, Apple is among the biggest offenders and can truly claim what they are doing is legal. Meanwhile Americans keep reelecting the Congress that marches to the "lobby" drum and despite that those we elected are aiding and abetting the big corporations + the financial sectors. Yet the banks + the lawyers of those prestigious Washington law firms, who aid and abet the complexities that exist in the tax code legislation as passed by Congress, are always employed to add to what remains in place + have long-term careers to continue their devious aims. And it seems as if members of Congress are accumulating fortunes they can "legally" protect by using the laws they created—if they are caught doing something that the everyday citizen can't do, they have nothing to fear as long as they are good loyal members of the party in power. For example, New York City Congressman Rangle received a "censure" for wrongly not declaring taxable assets, but he is expected to be reelected by the party machine that springs into action whenever there is an election coming up.

As for all of the above, I'm using my bully "thinkingoutloudan" pulpit to raise some important truths—for instance, the Government you elected is the Government that you have, because you aren't interested in asking for something better. It's as if you believe that our elected officials are doing the people's work when they initiate laws benefitting the Washington "K Street" crowd. And consider that all Americans below the top 1% are being left by the wayside when it comes to 21st century technological advances unless they take on debt to participate, and despite the claim "We are the party of the middle class" maintained as a mantra by the political party who controls the Senate and the Presidency. You should also remember this was the political party most interested in enacting "legacy" legislation + legislation that promises to bring more new voters to their ranks, thanks to a quasi open border policy.

ARE YOU EMPOWERED??? Cynthia Lynn

Isn't it time to elect for change???
To be continued...
2013

The litany recount of what needs to be done to bring about an equal playing field for the "every person" not just the top 1% sprung to the forefront the other day when I spoke to a manager at a local Office Supply chain store about a headset for my cheapie pay as you go Walmart purchased phone. We also talked about the new telephones that are being sold for huge sums of money but sometimes are free for a "locked in rate plan" at a rate that isn't regulated. He told me that he spends most of his money keeping current with telecommunications. "I'm a manager," he said. "I have to keep up with it." And he informed me about the $500 IPhone he bought with his credit card. "It's 3 years old but I am still paying for it," he said. When I suggested that he was spending money he didn't have, he declared, "I know but I have to keep current."

Although my chatty manager gets paid above the minimum wage, Office Supply chains don't pay their Manager employees a top 5 figure salary either. According to a recent article written by Elizabeth Olson in *The New York Times,* entitled, "Shaking Pennies and Fists Against Utility Rate Increases," the public is in somewhat apathetic attendance at the PSC rate increase meetings and the numbers who attend has fallen off considerably. Ms. Olson stated in her article that the AARP has started a campaign to alert citizens about the necessity of speaking out. She exampled South Carolina, whose citizens were successful in galvanizing public support about a 16% rate increase proposed by Duke. As a result the PSC of that state took notice and the rate increase was

ARE YOU EMPOWERED???   Cynthia Lynn

lowered to 10%. So far no one in the American Press or Consumer Activist groups have addressed the problem of why electric companies can recover expenses for servicing their utility. Or why electricity providers receive legal approval for not doing their job of maintaining their infrastructure. Nor do any of the "members of the powerful Press" care to redirect my conscience to explore the reason why electric utilities get to add a profit that pays dividends to their shareholders. Here's another fact of inequality that those members of the "powerful Press" fail to explore despite that they know the US middle class is unable to prosper while mired down with paying for electric providers rate increases approved by the utility regulators. And those "economists" who wear another hat: "member of the powerful Press" never write about how Americans are prevented by Federal Reserve policy from earning more than 1% and a few points interest on long term Federally insured CD bank savings accounts.

    I don't hear members of the "powerful Press" direct my conscience to the fact that banks charge the going rate for a mortgage + adds on service charges. Nor do these "powerful Press" + "dual hat economist" berate the Fed that allows banks to borrow at 0% and charge credit card interest up to 17.5 %. It's plain to see that the USA is a nation of borrowers who use credit cards to pay for living expenses and then pay the minimum to keep on living above their means, to pay for their bling necessities of life. No US economist will explain why the US government has a tax policy of money coming in and rebates going out for tax credits to those who are not legalized, but are holders of a tax ID and won't ever earn enough to pay taxes or pay for State

ARE YOU EMPOWERED???   Cynthia Lynn

and Local government services. I'm not an economist, though it's clear to me, the US Treasury needs its coffers full during the tax year to pay for "K Street" pork barrel and "legacy" legislation. Surely it has to be a win win for the IRS, since the Fed has been printing more money. I suppose that's why the IRS also keeps changing the rules regarding how much income qualifies for income tax credits. And I also realized that with its current "taxes in" and "rebate out" policy, the IRS is creating a legion of "tax preparers" who specialize in "rebate returns," but at least the IRS gets tax money from them. Yet too many in the barely left middle class are barely getting by + are falling into the dreaded Alternate Minimum Tax. Of course IRS knows that keeping any money from the "illegals" is not possible under our current income tax laws, so it grabs the unwary "barely making it middle class" with that "ALT Minimum Tax." All the while the rich getting richer are the investors the Fed has blessed with a bull stock market + Congress has given them a tax rate riddled with loopholes—those who are budget knowledgeable to the "shadow budget" process, know that this "money in money out" accounting system powers this US of A. Perhaps that's why Congress deliberately legislates the "ALT Minimum Tax" income percentages on a renew year to year basis.

Isn't this the time for Americans to ponder and consider why this country is being governed by a Congress who isn't interested in protecting the legal citizens who elected them???

To be continued...

ARE YOU EMPOWERED??? Cynthia Lynn

2013
According to the recent book by Harvard Professor of Economics Sendhil Mullainathan and Princeton Behavioral Psychologist Eldar Shafir, the 21st century is so complex that "bandwith" keeps most of us from concentrating on anything but our daily living problems. In the USA this is also a nationwide problem, because we have no available "bandwith," due to the fact we have to perform the basics of living in a 21st century technology society with new technologies constantly challenging us to keep up. Most Americans can't think of taking precious time to pressure Congress to help out with regulations that offer telecommunications services at a fair price. Which is why Americans cannot keep up with the necessities that enable us to exist in this 21st century. As well, Congress uses all of its "bandwith" to help the Washington "K street" lobby groups enact laws that speak to the big corporate donors and certain industries who receive favored treatment—such as the health care folks, who are "glad handing" donations to the political party that rammed the bonanza to the health care industry—which tacks on profits for its shareholders that US taxpayers must also subsidize, in addition, those of us who don't income qualify for a subsidy are double paying.

To date Americans have failed to question Government about too many things. It so happens the politicians keep talking about helping the "middle class," yet they have failed to legislate the circumstances to bring back a middle class society in America. Instead Government has encouraged the kind of trade that isn't "fair to America" trade, so says *The New York Times* "Op-ed" contributor Paul

ARE YOU EMPOWERED???   Cynthia Lynn

Greenberg, author of the forthcoming book *American Catch: The Fight for Our Local Seafood*. He asks, "Why Are Americans Importing Their Own Fish?" and he notes: "The seafood industry is a great example of the delete-and-replace maneuvers that define the outsourced American economy."

When it comes time for Americans to cast ballots for legislators who are indifferent to the fact that countries in Western Europe were saved by the American Marshal Plan yet have basic guarantees for their citizens not available in the USA. American voters should also ask how German private industry not only exists, as well makes profits that are reasonable, and does so despite that industry can't fire anyone without due cause + German productivity is more than in the USA. American voters also shouldn't forget that the Germans along with fellow Western Europeans enjoy a higher standard of living than average Americans. While here in this US of A, the top 1% enjoy all the bling available in this 21st century gilded age.

Here's another skewed fact: currently, the telecommunications giant AT&T isn't sitting on the Presidential couch, but AT&T is now interested in improving the living standards of Americans by sponsoring a "nannodegree" with participating community colleges for the purpose of hiring technologically trained Americans. The "shadow government Silicon Valley" hasn't spoken up about giving endowment money for projects like the "nannodegree." What the "shadow government Silicon Valley" crowd are looking for are special visas to bring in graduates from India and other countries who educate and train their workforce.

ARE YOU EMPOWERED???   Cynthia Lynn

The Challenge to Stay EMPOWERED

empowered against powerful interests

On August 30, 2014, in *The New York Times* James C. McKinley Jr. wrote an inspiring article "Top State Judge Tightens Rules on Debt Collection" which detailed an attempt by a debt collector to collect on a debt that was never borrowed by the woman who was hounded to pay it—when she was served with a legal judgment that effectively would have wiped out her entire savings, the woman and her daughter sought out a legal help service to take the case. The Judge's decision was not only a vindication of justice for a bogus debt that was never proven to be valid, it was a victory for 2 EMPOWERED women who weren't afraid to stand up and fight a system taking advantage of the debt collection industry's ability to keep Congress from legislating strong consumer debt protections.

an Empowered Electorate

"Globally" connected citizens have to be watchful that their government is working for them, and not for the powerful intent on pursuing their own agenda. In the USA, big corporations use those "K Street" Lobby Groups to influence legislators who are not interested in doing the people's work. It is my hope that

ARE YOU EMPOWERED??? Cynthia Lynn

Americans will finally decide it is time for a change.

an empowered network

For those who live in a nation where democratic laws and principles need to be expanded, only the EMPOWERED launch a network of the like-minded to get it done, but they need fortitude to keep government's feet to the fire of doing the people's work.

fully EMPOWERED

You are in control of your money, and you are ready to make those life-style changes that grant you the freedom to fearlessly step toward a new direction, and to pursue what you never thought was possible.

INDEX

Page

A
Action Plan..19
an empowered electorate....................154
an empowered network......................155
Another Suggestion..........................42
B
C
"Consumer Advocates"........................38
Consumer Friendly Fed........................40
Consumer Topics that Need
                Action..................128-9
D
E
empowered against powerful
                interests.............154
EMPOWERMENT.......................................124-5
ESSENTIALS..19
F
Federal Programs...................................23
FIND OUT how-to INTERNET TOPIC
                SEARCH..................36-7
        for the computer savvy................35-6
fully empowered......................................155
G
H
How To take Control of your life.............17-8
HOW DID YOU BECOME
                EMPOWERED.........124
I
INCOME NET...19
Inspired to Action..126-7
INTERNET TIPS..35-7
J
K
L

ARE YOU EMPOWERED??? **Cynthia Lynn**

let's sum up..18,31, 124-5

M
More about Your Network...................20-2, 35

more re QUESTIONS and Answers......................45

N
"Nolo's Law Blogs"..62

O

P
POINTERS plus HOW TO..........................33
Preface..11

Q
QUESTIONS..29-31

R

S
Selected Edited "thinkoutloudan" blogs............130
Schedule a Network Meeting.....................44-5
SECTION ONE..13-31
SECTION TWO......................................32-122
SECTION THREE..................................123-154
SOCIAL..19
Some popular USA Federal Programs....................23
Start the Empowerment Process.................................17

T
TEST your knowledge QUESTIONS and Answers........................44-
the 3 category Lists..................................19
the basics..14-5
The Challenge to Stay Empowered..................157-8
the How-To..17
the Process..18
the process of Change.............................28-9
The Sum Up..43
TIME OFF..19

ARE YOU EMPOWERED???   Cynthia Lynn

TIPS to keep in mind............................26-7
TOPIC 1. food...46-9
TOPIC 2. monthly mortgage
            (or rent)........................50-62
TOPIC 3. heating/cooling.........................63-9
TOPIC 4. commute....................................70-8
TOPIC 5. health insurance/
            other insurance.................79-88
TOPIC 6. banking-credit/debit
                        cards........................89-95
TOPIC 7. cellphone or landline.................96-100
TOPIC 8. TV/cable or satellite................101-5
TOPIC 9. internet....................................106-9
TOPIC 10. clothing/other
                        purchases..............110-5
TOPIC 11. charity donations...................116-8
TOPIC 12. religious tithe.......................119-22
U
V
W
what does empower mean?....................16
Why's and Wherefores about TEST
        Your Knowledge................................44
www.acf.hhs.gov/programs/
            ocs/liheap...............................65
www.attys.org/us-attorney-
            generals..................................84,86,
                    111,113,116
www.bankrate.com/the-basics-of
        private-mortgage-insurance..............50
www.charitynavigator.org/
            index.cfm.................................116
www.citizen.org/Page..............................40-1
www.consumeraffairs.com/
        news04/2012/06/utility-
        surcharges-fees..................................67
www.consumerfinance.gov........................93,111
www.creditcards.com/credit-
        card-news/dispute-credit
                        card..........................93

ARE YOU EMPOWERED???   Cynthia Lynn

www.csbs.org...56
www.denverpost.com/politics/
	ci_267501/Obama-
		annonces..............................95
www.dfi.wa.gov/consumers/
	education/debit............................110
www.dot.gov..38,75
www.economywatch.com/
		banks........................90
www.ehow.com/about_4596486
	_is-tithing-biblical...........................120
www.ehow.com/about_4679788
	_what-definition-tithing..................120
www.ehow.com/about_5372846
	_kind-tvs-digital-
		tuners........................103
www.ehow.com/about_
	5326702_term-vs-whole
	life-insurance..83
www.ehow.com/facts_
		5776611.......................91
www.ehow.com/facts_
		6087949_tithing...................120
www.ehow.com/facts_6154016_
	regulates-cell-phone
		companies...................96
www.ehow.com/how_2049261
		_get-charity-receipt..............118
www.ehow.com/how_5743758_
		file-complaint-cell-phone-
		company................................96
www.ehow.com/info_8623857.................24-5
www.ehow.com/info_
		78522365......................................60
www.ehow.com/issues-
		landlords........................53
www.ehow.com/list_7349199.....................118
www.electric.com/deregulation-
		of-energy...................137
www.farmaid.org/site...................................48-9

www.fcc.gov/complaints...............................97
www.fcc.gov/contact-us.............................98-9,
           100-1,103,105,107-9
www.fdic.gov..89
www.fhwa.gov/congestion/
      state_information..............................77
www.fns.usda.gov....................................24,46,
            48
www.freemoneyfinance.com/
      2007/02/how_to_tithe.....................119
www.healthcare.gov......................................85,87
www.helpwithmybank.gov..........................50,52,
         55,79, 92,94,113
www.hud.gov rental assistance..................60
www.hud.gov.portal/topics/
      buying_a_home......................58
www.irs.gov/uac/Contact-Your
      Local-IRS-Office..................................117
www.irs.gov/Businesses/Small-
      Businesses-&-Self-Employed/
      StateLinks1..117,
          122
www.medicare.gov..85
www.medicare.gov/claims-and-
          appeals....................86
www.medicare.gov/forms-
      help-and-resources........................87
www.medicare.gov-sign-up-
 change-plans/get-drug-
          coverage...................88
www.myrateplan.com/sat/
          condos....................105
     condoswww.naca.net......................42
www.naic.org/state_web_map..................79
          81,84
www.naruc.org/Coimmissions...................96,
      98,100-2,104,106,108-9
www.ncsl.org/research/transportation/
      registration-and-title-fees
          by-state.................................70

www.nolo.com legal encyclopedia
    renters rights........................61
www.personalinsure.about.
    com/od/auto........................81-2
www.sec/investor/pubs/certfic..................91
www.snap-help,com..................................46-7
www.tithing.com/blog/top-10-
    reasons-why-tithing-is-not-
    required....................119
www.usa.gov/directory/
    consumerorgs.......................40,
    56, 68
www.usa.gov/topics/money/
    banking/atm-debit................95
www.uslaw.com/library/Estate_
    Planning/Tithing_Gifts_
    Church_Valid_Receipt.....................122
www.wikipedia.org/wiki/
    Banking_in_the_United
    States........................90
www.wikipedia.org/wiki/
    Competitive_loccal_exchange
    _carrier.................................99
www.wikipedia.org/wiki/
    Department_of_Motor_
    Vehicles........................71
www.wikipedia.org/wiki/Employer
    _transportation_bvenefits_in_
    the_United_States...............72
www.wikipedia.org/wiki/
    Department_of_Transportation
www.wikipedia.org/wiki/Public_ utilities_
    commission...63,
    65,67,69
www.wikipedia.org/wiki/Tithe.....................120

Y

You And Your Network.................................20
YOUR Government Agencies............................26
    27,33-4

Z

YOUR NOTES

www.ingramcontent.com/pod-product-compliance
Lightning Source LLC
Chambersburg PA
CBHW050123020526
44112CB00035B/2368